M000029223

FINDING FLOW

Finding Flow

Spiritual Practices to Reclaim Inner Peace, Balance, and Wholeness

brian j. plachta

Paulist Press
New York / Mahwah, NJ

Scripture quotations are from the New Revised Standard Version Bible: Catholic Edition, copyright © 1989, 1993 National Council of the Churches of Christ in the United States of America. Used by permission. All rights reserved worldwide.

Cover image "inRelation" by Ralph Annunziata, www.studionunzi.net
Cover design by Sharyn Banks
Book design by Lynn Else

Copyright © 2022 by Brian J. Plachta
Author is represented by The Christopher Ferebee Agency, www.christoperferebee.com

Spiritual Gifts Inventory in the appendix used with permission from Neal Boese and Patricia Haller.

All rights reserved. No part of this publication may be reproduced, stored in a retrieval system, or transmitted in any form or by any means, electronic, mechanical, photocopying, recording, scanning, or otherwise, without either the prior written permission of the Publisher, or authorization through payment of the appropriate per-copy fee to the Copyright Clearance Center, Inc., www.copyright.com. Requests to the Publisher for permission should be addressed to the Permissions Department, Paulist Press, permissions @paulistpress.com.

Library of Congress Cataloging-in-Publication Data
Names: Plachta, Brian J., author.
Title: Finding flow : spiritual practices to reclaim inner peace, balance, and wholeness / Brian J. Plachta.
Description: New York/Mahwah, NJ : Paulist Press, 2022. | Summary: "Finding Flow is a popularly written spiritual formation book that is both anciently rooted and endlessly adaptive for today's readers"—Provided by publisher.
Identifiers: LCCN 2021023946 (print) | LCCN 2021023947 (ebook) | ISBN 9780809155576 (paperback) | ISBN 9781587689550 (ebook)
Subjects: LCSH: Spiritual life—Catholic Church. | Spirituality—Catholic Church. | Spiritual formation—Catholic Church.
Classification: LCC BX2350.3 .P567 2022 (print) | LCC BX2350.3 (ebook) | DDC 248.4/82—dc23
LC record available at https://lccn.loc.gov/2021023946
LC ebook record available at https://lccn.loc.gov/2021023947

ISBN 978-0-8091-5557-6 (paperback)
ISBN 978-1-58768-955-0 (e-book)

Published by Paulist Press
997 Macarthur Boulevard
Mahwah, New Jersey 07430
www.paulistpress.com

Printed and bound in the
United States of America

To my wife, Denise,
soulmate, best friend—the one who makes my heart sing.
Also to my spiritual friend, Ralph Annunziata,
who inspires me to grow and reminds me of whose I am.
Your lives and unconditional love continue to
show me how amazing God is.
And finally to the Divine Muse—the Creator—who inspires
me, co-creates in and through me, and teaches me
how to live into who I am.

Advance Reviews

Finding Flow shares the simplicity of spiritual practice in so many varied, longstanding, and proven ways that you will find yourself asking, "Why haven't I included such approaches to God in my life before?" Moving through the chapters, you will find yourself building your own tailored "rule of prayer" until you slowly move to develop a center of prayer within. This will set your spiritual life in motion so daily life can turn into a true pilgrimage marked by the resilience, inner peace, and compassion that can only come from a real relationship with God.

—Robert J. Wicks, author, *Heartstorming:*
Creating a Place God Can Call Home

Are you stuck in the mud...of the boring ordinary? brian plachta will hand you a shovel, lend you a hand, and help you find your way out with images and stories and the power of faith. brian has mined the experiences of his life and offers them to you to find your own way to balance and peace.

—Diane Zerfas, OP, coordinator for spirituality,
Dominican Center at Marywood

I am honored to enthusiastically endorse *Finding Flow*. brian plachta has written a delightful and helpful guide for practical ways to find one's spiritual and life-giving flow in everyday life. Especially appreciated are the personal stories of struggles to discern his vocation between becoming a priest and becoming a lawyer–husband–father–spiritual director–teacher of spirituality. brian flows with confidence between talking about the urgency of silence and Jung's concepts of the true and false selves to planning a "play-date" with God. I highly recommend *Finding*

FINDING FLOW

Flow for those seeking a "jump start" in their quest for a deeper relationship with our unconditionally loving God.

—Fr. Joachim Lally, CSP, spirituality workshop presenter and leader of missions to the Dominican Republic

Finding Flow communicates brian's deep desire for readers to cultivate a deep love relationship with the Divine. brian offers gentle, playful, and down-to-earth engagements with the Holy that will nourish the hearts of Christians yearning to be "rooted in an intimate relationship with the God of Love." He thoughtfully comingles ancient spiritual practices with activities such as sitting with God and a cup of coffee, going for a hike, and cultivating good friendships. This book will be soothing balm for Christians weary of intellectual argument and theological debate, who yearn to grow deeper in love with their Creator God.

—Matt Whitney, spiritual director, creative director of Spiritual Directors International, and host of *Encounters* SDI podcast

plachta's book is a delight, both captivatingly written and full of practical ideas to try. plachta writes from his own life with authenticity and courage and offers a deeply joyful and transforming path. Highly recommended.

—Paul Smith, author, *Integral Christianity* and *Is Your God Big Enough? Close Enough? You Enough?*

In his new book, brian plachta shares candidly from his personal faith journey to capture our attention and teach us about finding "the flow," or as he notes: letting it find us. By "flow," brian refers to "inner peace, balance and wholeness" through various forms of prayer to a loving God. brian's writing style is relatable, allowing us to grasp a wide variety of practical, spiritual practices. We are invited to discover which work best for us given where we are in our own faith journey. I wish I had brian's book when I was thirty but am glad to have it at age sixty-two.

—Bill Lawrence, attorney, businessman, community volunteer

Contents

Acknowledgments

A heartfelt thanks to my agent, Chad R. Allen, who believed in *Finding Flow* each step of the way. Chad, you are a gift to me and so many other writers. Thanks for helping me find my voice. I also want to thank Christopher Ferebee for his work with Paulist Press. And a hat's off to my long-time editor, Sandy Tritt, who shapes and molds my writing with her loving and wise wordsmithing. Thank you also to all the great folks at Paulist Press, including Diane Vescovi, who helped bring *Finding Flow* into the world. Finally, thank you to Don Heydens, my spiritual director. Your guidance and God's grace continue to help me hear the whisper of the Holy Spirit.

Part One

SOLITUDE

Not all of us are called to be hermits, but all of us need enough silence and solitude in our lives to enable the deeper voice of our own self to be heard.

—Thomas Merton

Introduction

I'm scared—a lot.

I'm scared of roller coasters, bears, being late for work, criticism, crashing my car, loved ones dying, getting cancer, having a heart attack, shark attacks, screwing up, and mean people. Just to name a few.

God was someone I also used to fear. But not anymore.

Creepy Fear

My first memory of fear is the day I entered preschool and realized the world isn't always safe. With my backpack snug to my shoulders, I pulled open the school doors. The clamor of metal bells exploded near my head attacking me. I froze, closed my eyes, and glued my hands to my ears.

I never wanted to go back to school after that day. I feared that angry school bell was out to get me. In my childlike mind, those school bells had metal arms ready to reach out and grab me and lock me in the janitor's closet with a towel stuffed in my mouth. I didn't realize my fear was rooted in normal separation anxiety.

Mom told me that night, "You need to stop being afraid."

But I didn't know how. There wasn't a switch I could flip to make the fear go away.

And it got worse as I grew into adulthood. Do I have enough money? Will my spouse abandon me? Did I remember to blow out the candle? Will I go to heaven?

3

Sometimes fear comes in different shapes and sizes. It's often disguised as free-floating anxiety. When that happens, there's nothing in particular I'm fearful about, I'm just skittish on the inside. Filled with nervous worry.

According to an article in PR Newswire,[1] 84 percent of Americans suffer from some form of fear or anxiety. Whether it's worrying about losing our jobs, failing as parents, or getting dementia, fear haunts us like those angry school bells.

Fear's like a monster. It tells us we're not safe, not loved, or—even worse—we're bad. And before you know it, we forget we're God's original blessing, the Beloved.

Understanding and Experiencing God

Growing up, I took the biblical phrase "Fear of the Lord is the beginning of wisdom" (Prov 9:10) literally. I thought I was supposed to cower before God. I was afraid he'd bop me on the head and send me to "H-E-double hockey sticks" if I stepped out of line and didn't follow all the right rules. My God was an old, angry man sitting on a throne somewhere in outer space ready to zap me with a cosmic thunderbolt if I didn't do what he demanded.

This type of fear-based spirituality got me stuck in my head, trying to think my way to God. I tried my best to follow all the rules, but I never felt I could please God enough.

All the intellectual stuff my parents and catechism teachers taught me about God provided a good spiritual foundation, and I'm grateful.

But I longed to experience God. Directly.

I wanted to take what I'd learned intellectually and integrate it into a real-life, God-with-skin relationship with the

Creator. I wanted to know what God felt like on the inside—in my heart.

I was afraid to enter into that kind of an intimate relationship with the Creator because my image of God was too small. I mean, seriously, who'd want to be a bosom-buddy with a mean old guy who's always angry at you?

So, I looked for another image of God. In the process, I learned that to grow spiritually we need to take the first part of knowing God intellectually and add the other part: direct experience of God.

As the Spirit nudges us into an ever-deepening relationship with the Creator, we're invited to encounter Divine Presence one-on-one like Jesus did. And as we do, we learn to trust that our spiritual experiences are real.

Jesus and His Dad

During his earthly life, Jesus not only learned about God by studying the Torah, listening to his parents, and sitting in the temple at the feet of wise teachers; he also had a direct relationship with his Father. He felt God's loving presence on the inside—in his heart.

Praying in the quiet each morning, he heard the Father remind him of his deep love. He got the game-plan for the day's work he'd been given to do and the courage to do it.

At his baptism, Jesus experienced the Real Presence of God, saying, "This is my Son, the Beloved, with whom I am well pleased" (Matt 3:17). At the transfiguration, Jesus conversed with Moses and Elijah, who explained what was about to unfold in the next phase of his life. And in the Garden of Gethsemane, Jesus talked with his Father, told him he was afraid, and God sent a messenger to give him the inner strength he needed to endure the cross.

I wanted the same experience of God that Jesus had during his earthly life. I wanted to move from a fear-based spirituality to one rooted in an intimate relationship with the God of love.

As I learned about the experiential part of faith, my initial understanding of God as someone to fear changed. I entered a new phase of spiritual growth. My pastor told me the Old Testament word *fear* can also be translated as "awe." Being awed by the infinite love and guidance of God is the beginning of wisdom, he said.

Pastor told me that the New Testament invites us to a deeper stage of spiritual growth. Jesus came to teach us that God is love. And he modeled that love by experiencing his Father's presence through daily times alone with his Dad. He showed us how much he loves us by the supreme act of dying, rising again, and placing the Holy Spirit in our hearts.

Like Jesus, we can experience God's guidance and encouragement because we are the expression of divine love in the world. We're called to live our lives co-creating with God.

Is Your Image of God Big Enough?

My image of God moved from a mean old angry judge whom I had to please to get what I wanted into an intimate relationship with the Source of my being.

I fell in love with God. I realized for the first time the Creator loves me unconditionally. He loves us all that way.

I learned God wants us to be happy, like any good parent desires for their children. The Divine Spirit is always moving in our lives, drawing us toward our highest good. Our job is to listen and discover the Spirit's movement so we can follow divine guidance and reclaim inner peace. That's how we move from a fear-based spiritually into a love-based relationship with God.

Doable Spiritual Practices

While there's not a switch that clicks off fear, I learned there are a number of doable spiritual practices we can adopt as a doorway into a deeper experience of God. These practices direct our focus away from fear and toward its antidote: love.

Our spiritual practices quiet our mind chatter, open our hearts, and refocus our attention inward, so we can receive whatever God wishes to offer us. We get into the flow of divine wisdom.

Over time, we recognize God's presence more easily, harness our fears, become more fully alive, and live as we've imagined is possible by leaning into the encouragement and guidance of a loving God who shows us the way.

Finding Flow

It's time to overcome fear and adopt a time-tested way to reclaim inner peace, balance, and wholeness. It's time to find flow—the kind of flow that connects us with God and our authentic selves, flow that's filled with divine energy, flow that leads to happiness. That's what I want for you. So let's get started.

1

Childlike Flow
Rediscover Life's Natural Rhythm

I loved rainstorms when I was five years old. Peering out my living room window, nose stuck to the glass, my heart pounded as I watched winds blow, trees bend, and gobs of water *splash* and *splatter* against the sidewalk.

I pulled on my lime-green rubber boots and pushed my arms into a yellow raincoat. I dashed out the front door and hugged my hood to my head as a driving rain pelted my face.

As the rain raged, I grabbed a stick, dragged it along the sidewalk, stopped, tilted my head, and tried to figure out why the water kept flooding into the street.

Soon, I spotted the culprit: bunched-up maple leaves stopping the water from flowing into the curbside drain.

Like a tiger cub, I pounced on the leaves with my stick, *Ker-plunk, nudge, poke.*

Raising my stick high as if I were Moses, I commanded, "Let the water *flow!*"

Leaves parted. Water gushed. My spirit splashed with joy.

I've often thought about that gutter as a metaphor for what happens to us as adults in our relationship with God. Fear, self-doubt, and the daily struggles of life are some of the leaves that choke off our connection with the One who made us and wants what's best for us.

If we don't clear the blockage, life can become unmanageable. We get confused. Anxious. Overwhelmed. Some people develop addictions to numb the pain of interior discontent and depression. Others feel the effects physically with problems such as diabetes, high blood pressure, and chronic heart conditions.

The Journey Back to Wholeness

I'm not sure when I lost that childlike connection between myself and God, the one I felt when I was young. Maybe the disconnect seeped in during my thirties. I'd pushed hard, getting my education, launching a legal career, searching for and marrying my wife and soulmate, and raising our family. I had a four-bedroom house on a hill and a golden retriever. I sent my kids to private schools and drove a Jeep Grand Cherokee with a sunroof I loved to open wide as I cruised city streets. I was living the life I'd imagined.

But something inside me didn't feel right. The daily duties expected of me as a lawyer and father became numbing. Overwhelming. I was ghosting through life.

I still went to church, but God became abstract, someone "out there," not "in here" as part of my life. I was drowning. My heart was clogged. Depression overshadowed me.

"You're stuck as that sixteen-year-old kid, standing at your father's graveside, watching as they lowered his casket into the ground," my counselor told me during one of our weekly sessions. "You need to join a support group for adults who've lost a parent as a child. You need to learn how to grieve your father's death."

That's when I met Gloria.

Gloria was part of the hospice support group I attended at my counselor's prodding. Gloria had also lost a parent when she was a child. As I listened, her words spoon-fed my soul.

"Don't push the river. Let the river flow," Gloria said. She was twisted pretzel-like in her wheelchair—hands, arms, and legs crippled with cerebral palsy. Her frail frame wrapped itself around a forty-three-year-old soul—one filled with a lifetime of wisdom—the kind that comes from great suffering transformed by Divine Love.

"Think back to when you were a child," Gloria said, putting me in the hotspot in front of the ten people sitting around a cloth-covered table. A flickering candle scented the air with vanilla.

"Is there a time in your past when you felt that rhythm, that natural flow like a gentle river, a sense of being connected, safe, and whole?" she pressed further.

I paused and pondered. As the group waited in silence, that childhood memory reappeared—the one of me as a five-year-old unclogging leaves in the gutter. For an instant, I was that tiger-cub kid again. As the memory flooded my imagination, I felt whole. Safe. Peaceful. One with myself and the Creator. A smile blushed my care-worn face. My heart softened. My lungs opened wide, tasting fresh air.

As I closed my eyes and savored the moment, my heart pleaded to the God I'd forgotten, "Let my life *flow* again."

That meeting with Gloria thirty years ago was the beginning of a journey to rediscover the childlike flow I'd lost as an adult. From that point on, I paid attention to flow. I studied it. I named it as such when I experienced it. When I was out of the flow, pushing the river or lost in life's whirlpools, I increased times of solitude to shake off the world and unclog the connection between God and me.

Shortly after meeting Gloria, I studied to become a spiritual director. As part of the coursework, we learned about saints and spiritual masters, including Saint Benedict.

Benedict, known as the father of Western monasticism, wrote a rulebook for monastic life in the sixth century to give his monks a template for finding balance between prayer and daily work (*ora et labora*). He called it a Rule of Life. The monks were required to follow the Rule as their guiding principles, a framework for finding inner peace and balance in their daily lives. Today, we might call it a personal mission statement.

As part of our three years of spiritual direction classes, we were tasked with the assignment to create our Rule of Life. As I pondered, I looked to the spiritual giants we studied. I noted how each man and woman—Saint Benedict, Saint Francis, Julian of Norwich, Saint Teresa of Avila, Jesus, and others—had four common lifestyle practices that shaped their lives.

First, they took daily time for solitude, to be alone with God—time to meditate and listen for the Whisper of the Holy Spirit.

Second, they read the writings of spiritual masters to gain insight and learn wisdom.

Third, they surrounded themselves with people who inspired them to grow, people who nudged and encouraged them to take another step outside of their comfort zone.

Finally, they did the inner work to discover their unique talents and gifts, to figure out what made them come alive. They then used those talents in life-giving ways for themselves and others.

I shaped my Rule of Life around the ancient wisdom of Benedict and the other spiritual masters. The following became my Rule, the guiding principles through which I seek inner peace, balance, and wholeness:

1. **Solitude:** taking quiet time each day to connect with myself and God
2. **Spiritual Reading:** studying the writings of others further along on the spiritual journey to discover the wisdom and guidance they offer

3. **Community:** surrounding myself with people who inspire and nudge me to grow
4. **Contemplative Action:** doing the necessary inner work to discover my unique talents and gifts and then using them in ways that are life-giving for myself and others

I call the above Rule of Life *Finding Flow*. I define *flow* as being one with the Divine Spirit who opens our hearts, allowing us to experience inner peace, balance, and wholeness.

This definition has several components.

First, it points to our heart's deepest desire: being loved and guided by God, the Source of our Being.

Second, it recognizes that it's the Holy Spirit and God's grace that opens our hearts. Our job is to create the inner space for Divine Love to grow.

Finally, it suggests that when we deepen our relationship with God, we experience inner peace, balance, and wholeness. We plug into the wisdom and guidance the Creator offers us.

I want to unfold these components with you through the stories in this book. They will serve as guideposts, helping us experience abiding joy.

I believe we can take Benedict's wisdom, even if we're not monks, and find unique ways to translate it into modern life. We can look at our lives through the lens of these guideposts to discover and reclaim wholeness. According to Robert Thiefels, in his book *Standing in the Midst of Grace*,[1] we are already whole because we're patterned in God's image and share God's likeness. We've just forgotten that truth. So, we need to find a way to remember and live into the truth of who we already are—

individuals patterned by and created in the likeness of Divine Love.

Finding flow is a way we can reclaim our Divine Image. I've learned from the many mentors in my life that finding flow involves adopting and integrating into our daily lives spiritual practices, several of which I'll share in this book.

As you'll discover in the pages that follow, daily solitude is key to finding flow. Mother Teresa underscores that fact: "In the silence of the heart God speaks. If you face God in prayer and silence, God will speak to you."[2]

A History of Flow

In 1975, Mihály Csíkszentmihályi introduced the concept of flow as a psychological theory, though the idea has existed for thousands of years under other names, notably in some Eastern religions such as Buddhism. The term has become a common buzzword for athletes who describe themselves as being "in the zone" when they're immersed in their sport. Artists, writers, and other creatives also speak of "being in the flow" when their art pours out with effortless joy.

To date, the conversation about flow has been limited to its artistic, psychological, and athletic components. Writers such as Frank Van De Ven,[3] who try to define what getting into the flow means, seem to skip discussion about flow's spiritual element.

However, we miss a lot by not recognizing that flow involves our whole being—mind, body, *and* spirit. When I was that five-year-old kid unclogging leaves in the gutter, my mind, body, and spirit were fully immersed in flow. I may not have identified it as such back then, but I was having a spiritual experience. I felt it in the marrow of my bones. I trusted it. It filled me with joy and bliss.

As an adult, I still get that natural *let-the-river-flow* feeling whenever I grab a stick during a rainstorm and unplug the leaves in the gutter. It's the same feeling I experience when I sit in quiet meditation and sense God and me connecting.

Divine Flow

How about we add to our conversation about flow its spiritual element? Maybe give it a name like "Divine Flow"? Christians call it the *Holy Spirit*. Others say it's karma, the Great Spirit, or Divine Love.

Franciscan priest Richard Rohr in *Breathing under Water* writes, "It is no surprise at all that our common metaphors for the Holy Spirit all honor and point to a kind of flow experience: living water, blowing wind, descending flames, and alighting doves."[4]

Whatever you call it, however you describe it, flow points to this universal truth: the Infinite Being—our Creator—loves and guides us with unconditional love and wisdom, and we can connect with Being.

How Do We Find Flow?

Over the years, I've learned that finding Divine Flow takes inner work and daily practice. Just like going to the gym and working out maintains healthy bodies, regular spiritual practices sustain healthy souls.

As those practices become a habit, eventually we look into our life's rearview mirror and notice our hearts have opened. Our relationship with God has deepened. We've discovered more inner peace, balance, and wholeness. Unconditional love for ourselves and others overflows. We find divine guidance. Wisdom. It's as if we've found our Inner Compass.

My buddy Ralph asked me several years ago, "How do you find flow?" I don't know if I have ever found flow, but what follows in the next chapters are some of the ways flow found *me*.

2

"Hang on, Jesus, We're Going for a Ride!"

What's Your Name for God?
What's God's Name for You?

When I was a kid, I looked for God everywhere, like looking for Waldo in *Where's Waldo?* children's books. But it wasn't Waldo I was trying to find—it was God. Looking for the Creator was fun.

I looked for him in trees, in birds, in sunshine. And I talked to him like he was my best friend.

Sometimes I pretended Jesus was a superhero sitting on my shoulder. He and I would run outdoors, play, and explore the world together, climbing maple trees and building forts. I loved hanging out with God. We even had nicknames for each other. God called me his "buddy." I called God my "friend."

At night when I knelt next to my bed to say prayers, I often took a quick peek underneath the bed, thinking maybe God was right there just beyond the brown comforter that skirted the floor. I hoped he was saying his prayers with me.

I sometimes imagined he winked back from the dust-covered floor beneath my bed. And then I'd pretend to scoop him into my arms, pull back my sheets and comforter, and tuck him in bed with me, right next to Curious George and Raggedy Andy.

I think God liked hanging out with me. I know I felt safe in my bed as I fell asleep on his imaginary shoulder.

Sometimes I got into trouble talking to my best friend God and his son Jesus. Like the time I was in church.

I was playing with my mom's rosary during Mass and thought Jesus looked sad hanging there all stiff on the cross at the end of the beads. I decided to do something about it.

"Hang on, Jesus, we're going for a ride!" I shouted in the middle of the priest's homily as I twirled the blue rosary high above my head. The spanking I got when we arrived home was well worth making Jesus happy that day.

Learning about and Experiencing God Directly

As I grew older and learned about God through Bible studies and religion classes, it seemed like I lost God somewhere. I don't know when and where exactly, but he lived far outside of me instead of on my shoulder like my best friend.

The older I became, the more I got stuck trying to intellectualize my way to God instead of experiencing him. All the dogma and doctrine I learned about God through catechism class and the other ideas I picked up as I matured seemed to get all jammed up in my head.

I know we need to learn about God so we can better understand ourselves and him, but I get confused sometimes with all the theory. I just want to experience God like I did when I was a kid—directly, trusting him and myself. I want to touch and feel God's hands, know he's real. I want to feel he's connected to my story and I'm connected to his. I want to feel certain that Jesus and I are hanging out, that we're on life's ride together.

A Three-Legged Stool

In her book *The Wisdom Way of Knowing*, Cynthia Bourgeault writes that Western culture has tried to reason its way to God. By doing so, we've reduced God to theological theories. We try to stuff him into a couple of concepts or memorized Bible verses so we can put him into our mental box.

But God is much larger than our intellect. God is a relationship of love among the Creator, others, and us.

According to Bourgeault, the Creator gives us three receptors connected through our hearts with which we're invited to experience him: the mind, the emotions, and the body. When we have all three of our sensors operating together, we connect with the Divine in real and experiential ways.

Bourgeault suggests our souls have been gifted with a three-centered knowing—intellectual center, emotional center, and movement center—all active, working, and cooperating together to connect us with God.[1]

I imagine these centers like a three-legged stool. When all three legs are in place, they provide balance and stability. Harmony.

This "experiential knowing" allows our mind, emotions, and body to work together so we can fully experience life. For example, when we watch the sunrise, our emotions flood with wonder and awe as we stare at its beauty. Our skin feels the warmth of the sun's rays nurturing our body with vitamin D. And our mind recognizes the amazing gift sunlight gives us each day.

Maybe this three-centered way of knowing describes the childlike simplicity I experienced as a kid. Perhaps when I was climbing trees, twirling rosaries, and tucking Jesus into bed with me, my three-legged stool was fully balanced.

My emotions overflowed with joy and laughter as I climbed trees with God. I felt safe and secure as I lay my head on the pillow next to him each night. My body sensed his physical presence as the energy of his love radiated through my limbs. As I swung Jesus around on the rosary, I felt his touch on my heart like a gentle breeze smiling on the inside of my chest. And I allowed my mind with its youthful imaginings to live in awe of the mystery of God's presence. I was free from the adult trap of overthinking. My mind was open to imagination and enjoying God's real presence in my life.

Sometimes as an adult I still get all jammed up overthinking God. I forget to experience God. I forget how to feel the Creator's presence through my emotions and body. I stop using my imagination to connect with him. I forget that the language of God is experiential, not intellectual.

What's Your Name for God? What's God's Name for You?

One way to return to *experiencing* God is to rediscover our names for the Creator and the Creator's names for us, using the three-centered knowing of our minds, bodies, and emotions. Allowing our imaginations to run free and consider what God calls us and what we call God helps us reclaim our childlike relationship with the Creator.

In the last few years, I've begun taking time each day to sit in silence and get in touch with my emotions by really feeling them, naming them, and then talking with God about them. As I do, a calm cascades over my body. The inner tension wanes. My jaw relaxes. I listen to my breathing. My heart opens. I feel a sense of flow, a sense of being connected with the Divine. And I've come to trust those experiences as the real presence of God.

Slowly, I'm understanding this three-centered way of knowing God is key to deepening my relationship with him and with myself. I'm returning to that childlike way of experiencing the Creator without intellectualizing him. It feels like my Best Friend and I are on this ride of life again. Together.

The practice of connecting with mind, body, and emotions has opened my heart to the freedom of asking the questions once again: Who is God to me? Who am I to God? These questions shape and mold our unfolding relationship with the Creator and ourselves. They allow us to live into the answers.

I no longer climb maple trees with God or swing him around on rosary beads, but my lived experience of the Divine has allowed me to see his presence in me, in others, and in all Creation. Today I call him "Creator." And in moments of quiet contemplation, I hear him call me "Beloved son."

Take some time to sit in silence and ask yourself, "What's my name or image of God? What's God's name or image for me?"

3

Escaping the Tsunami

Schedule a Playdate with God

"Put down your cell phone. It's dinnertime," my wife said as I peeked at emails popping up on my iPhone between bites of chicken and mashed potatoes. "The office can wait."

I shook my head and sighed as I put the phone back into my pocket. "I'm overwhelmed," I said. "Between work, the kids, house chores, volunteering, and everything else on my plate, I feel like I'm in a tsunami, barely keeping my head above the waves of responsibilities. I'm drowning."

"Why don't you take a God-date?" my wife suggested. "Put an appointment on the calendar for you and God to go hang out. Go for a long run, a walk, take a hike. Create some space in your calendar for something that's life-giving. When you come back, you'll be refreshed and able to love me, the kids, and your work with a renewed spirit."

My spiritual mentor had suggested the same that week. "Can you give yourself permission each month to take a day or even half a day for a playdate with God?" she asked. "Clear your calendar. Don't let anything get in the way."

Go Play!

The importance of play for children is well-documented, says psychiatrist Stuart Brown, founder of the National Institute for Play. We ensure schoolchildren have adequate snack and recess times. We use play therapy when a child suffers trauma. Play helps youngsters gain social skills and release pent-up energy. Some of our lifelong childhood friends were made on the playground.

Researchers are now turning their attention to the benefits of play for adults. What they're finding is that it isn't just about goofing off. It can also be an important means for reducing stress and helping us develop an overall sense of well-being. Saying "Goodbye, responsibility" as we head out the door for a weekend camping trip can be better therapy—and less expensive—than sitting in a counselor's office.

"What all play has in common is that it offers a sense of engagement and pleasure, takes the player out of a sense of time and place, and the experience of doing it is more important than the outcome," says Brown.[1] Whether it's jumping in a mudpuddle, building sandcastles at the beach, or reading a favorite book, play allows us to regain our childlike spirits.

In a *Washington Post* article, "Why It's Good for Grown-Ups to Go Play," Jennifer Wallace reports, "Play is a basic human need as essential to our well-being as sleep. When we don't take time to rejuvenate ourselves with play, we get cranky, rigid, feel stuck in a rut or victimized."[2] The "poor-me" syndrome overshadows our adult lives. We lose our sense of joy.

Let Me Entertain Me

Lynn Barnett, a professor of recreation, sports, and tourism at the University of Illinois, says playful adults transform everyday situations—even stressful ones—into something entertaining. She coauthored a study that found highly playful adults—those who rated themselves as being spontaneous or energetic and open to clowning around—reported less stress in their lives because they've developed better coping skills. They keep stress in perspective.

Barnett theorizes, "Highly playful adults feel the same stressors as anyone else, but they appear to experience and react to them differently, allowing stressors to roll off more easily than those who are less playful."[3]

How we play is as unique to an individual as a fingerprint. It could mean collecting stamps, tossing a football, knitting, or climbing Mount Everest, says Brown.

For painters, writers, and other creatives, taking time for fun reconnects them with their inner muse, Julia Cameron says in *The Artist's Way*. She calls these creative escapades an "Artist's Date" and suggests we indulge in them weekly.

Steve, a minister, began his regular God-dates a year ago. Each month he pencils in his playtime on the calendar. He goes for a hike in the woods, takes a walk alongside a river, or rides his bike. His God-dates have become so life-giving he preaches their importance to his congregation.

Choosing the Tsunami

For some reason—perhaps our need to feel productive or to please others—the last person we put on our to-do lists is ourselves. We resist taking time to be alone and play like we did as children.

Why is that? Maybe we don't feel worthy of taking time for ourselves. We were taught it's better to give than to receive. So we neglect our needs out of guilt. We put others first to the point of exhaustion. Perhaps we think it's selfish to love ourselves—but that's not what Christ taught.

Christ summarized the long list of Old Testament rules with a New Testament command: love God, love others, *and* love ourselves. We often get the loving God and others right, but the daily grind crowds out room for ourselves. We get the short end of our to-do list.

The problem is, when this happens, a growing sense of distraction or even resentment churns inside us like surging waves until a full-blown tsunami erupts and we come out sideways—nervously checking our phones at the dinner table or even blowing up at loved ones.

We have to face the fact that when we neglect ourselves, we're choosing the tsunami.

To be whole, we need time to fill our tanks—taking time for solitude so we can love ourselves well. We rediscover an inner freedom in our alone time. As we regain that childlike spirit, we fall in love with ourselves again.

J.C. Thomas

I took my wife's advice and put a monthly appointment on my calendar with God. On my work calendar, I call it an appointment with "J.C. Thomas," so I don't have to explain it to anyone. I told my office and family not to schedule anything during that time. It's a sacred priority.

When my God-date gets closer, I ask the Creator and myself a simple question: "What do you want to do, buddy? What would be life-giving?" Then I go with my gut and do what's fun and adventurous—something that feels like play.

Sometimes I go to a favorite park or take a long walk along a pebbled riverbed. Other times I go to church and sit alone in the quiet. Often a bike ride through rural roads is just what I need to relax and recharge.

Scripture tells us that Jesus often wandered into the desert or hillside to be alone with his Father. While healing a group of villagers, he even stopped and retreated to a quiet place when he realized he'd run out of energy. He needed time to be alone and recharge.

If Jesus took God-dates to escape the tsunami, maybe I can give myself permission to do likewise.

Maybe you can too.

4

Quiet Time Solves Everything

Create Space for Daily Solitude—
Connect with Yourself and the Creator

"How do I grow spiritually?" I asked Casey, the attorney-turned-lay-evangelist, at the end of a week-long mission at my church.

I was in my early thirties and recently elected partner at my law firm. Our four children were doing well in school. My wife was happy being a homemaker. I served on the parish council and building committee. I was working sixty hours a week and went to Mass every Sunday with my family.

But something was missing. I felt empty. I was ghosting through life again.

After my law firm announced I'd made partner, I took a day off to celebrate. The shores of Lake Michigan are my favorite place to chillax, so I got up early, packed a lunch, grabbed a beach towel, and headed to the lake. At first, I was excited and grateful, but those feelings soon faded when a too familiar nagging emptiness came back to haunt me.

"*Really*?" I pondered as my back rested against the warm sand. "Is this what grabbing the brass ring of success looks like? Nothing's really changed, except now I owe the law firm thirty thousand dollars to buy stock. Where's that money going to come from?" A scowl grimaced my face.

What should have been a joyous celebration soon became a dark lament as I wondered, "Is this *all* there is to life?"

I met Casey several days later.

The Power of Slowing

Casey was also a lawyer, but he'd given up his day job to become what he called a full-time "Catholic Lay Evangelist." Our church hired him to preach a mission for five nights on how to deepen our relationship with God. Being the good Catholic I felt compelled to be, my wife and I attended the evening sessions.

By the middle of the week, Casey's words stirred something deep within my gut. I didn't know what it was. I struggled to give it a name.

It felt like I was encountering a Presence—or maybe that Presence was encountering me. It was seeking me, wanted to beckon, guide, teach, heal, and show me deeply who I am.

All my life I had longed for an experience of God beyond mere intellectual knowledge. When Casey told us the Creator of the stars and galaxies—the One who forms us out of Infinite Love—wanted to communicate with us, I felt that Presence within my heart.

It was the same presence I'd read about in Gerald May's book *The Wisdom of Wilderness.*[1]

May says he also longed for a direct encounter with Divine Presence. He wanted to experience "that Something that is in you but not yet completely you—something dynamic, surprising, and very, very wise."[2] He was tired of the indirect, intellectual experience of God—a god who was something or someone "out there." It left him feeling separated from himself and the Divine.

May wanted to feel Presence rising from his deepest parts—to experience it inside his muscles, to feel the gentle hand of the Creator taking his arms and legs and stilling them. And most of all, he wanted to hear the Voice of Wisdom speak within him.

When diagnosed with incurable cancer and given months to live, May decided to spend time in quiet solitude each day. On weekends, he went alone and camped in the mountains. He sat in contemplation. Listening. Waiting. And after faithfully showing up for daily solitude, May experienced the Presence for which he longed. He heard the Voice of Wisdom within him.

He described it as a "sweet, irresistible voice speaking in my belly. It whispered, 'Be still now.' It's not a real voice, not actual hearing, but the message is clear: no rush, no need to do anything, just *be*."[3]

This Presence, what May called the *power of slowing*, guided him through his illness to the Other Side. I've never had cancer. But I often feel the same yearning May experienced. It was that yearning I felt while sitting in church listening to Casey.

Coffee with the Creator

After one of the evening sessions, I went up to Casey and asked him, "How do I grow spiritually? How do I connect with the Presence that seems to be stirring within me?"

"Quiet time solves everything," Casey said as he placed his fingers to his lips. "Sit quietly for twenty minutes each day. Let silence find you. Through the daily practice of solitude and meditation, you'll learn how to slow down, connect with your core self, and experience God's Divine Presence."

Casey's suggestion seemed a little too simplistic, but I decided to try it anyway. Before I went to bed that night, I set my alarm clock a half an hour earlier than usual, just like Casey told me to do.

The next morning when the alarm rang, I got out of bed, shuffled into the kitchen, made coffee, poured myself a mug, and instead of clicking on the news or social media, I went to my den. There I lit a candle, sat on my couch in the quiet— waiting, hoping, letting silence find me.

A mystical cloud didn't blanket me. An angel didn't appear to give me tidings of great joy. Instead, I simply felt comfort. Peace. It was as if I had entered a sacred space. My body sighed and relaxed. I opened my heart, connected with my soul, and wondered whether this is what having coffee with the Creator feels like.

As I sat in meditation, I thought about how Jesus rose daily. He stretched his limbs, lifted his bones from the ground, and sat silently, listening to his Father. In solitude, Jesus gained strength to meet the challenges of the day. The inner voice of the Spirit provided wisdom and guidance for his journey. Filled with the love his Father showered upon him in the quiet, Jesus rose and attended to the day's tasks.

Ever since that comforting morning in my den, I've made it a practice to set aside daily quiet time to be with God. I rise and have coffee with the Creator.

Life still has its ups and downs, but now I have an inner home, a sanctuary, a place I can go to each morning and throughout the day. In this spiritual home, I experience God's presence, guidance, and wisdom. Deep within my heart I feel the Holy Spirit's love.

According to the late Father Thomas Keating,[4] the growing popularity and return to the ancient practices of meditation and contemplation in our current age is the work of the Holy

Spirit—a sign of hope—an invitation to leave the noise and chaos of our busy lives and experience inner peace.

The Holy Spirit was definitely up to something when Casey popped into my life. Casey is right: quiet time solves everything, starting from within ourselves. Making quiet time a priority develops a deeper awareness of God within, an awareness of being deeply loved no matter what happens.

5

Give Your Monkey-Mind a Banana

Discover the Gifts of Centering Prayer and Imaginary Prayer

During the first couple of mornings, my quiet time was awesome. I felt relaxed. My heart was peaceful. I imagined God was holding me, and as I did, I experienced the same Presence I felt that night at the church mission.

On the third morning, I swear a bunch of howler monkeys took up residence in my head. My thoughts kept racing: Why are you sitting here in the dark? Don't you have anything *better* to do? You're not very good at this meditation stuff, you know.

I kept thinking about all the things I had to do that day. I was ready to blow out the candle, leave the solitude of my den, head to the office, and tackle my to-do list.

But then I felt an inner nudge: Why don't you give Casey a call? See if he knows a way to quiet that monkey-mind.

I phoned Casey later that day and told him how restless I'd become that morning. "It was like a tribe of monkeys were chattering *ook! ook!* in my head as my thoughts kept grunting at me. And my inner voice howled, telling me I was a failure. How do I tame those noisy monkeys?" I asked Casey.

"Feed them a banana," he replied.

"What?"

"When your mind starts racing, give it something to chew on."

"Interesting. How do I do that?"

According to Casey, our minds can focus on only one thought at a time. If we give our minds something to chew on—like a word, phrase, or our breath—our minds will focus on it, stop rambling, and become quiet.

There are many pathways we can follow to anchor the mind during quiet time, Casey said. You can focus on your breath or your heartbeat. A prayerful walk or spending time in nature can be calming. Sitting in church before the Eucharist can also be a powerful way to focus our minds. Casey suggested two practices: centering prayer and imaginary prayer.

Centering Prayer

Centering prayer is a way to tame our chattering mind so we can enjoy inner peace and quiet. It's a gentle discipline that allows us to calm our minds and open our hearts so we can listen for the Creator's wisdom and guidance. Centering prayer invites us to simply rest in God.

Casey said the practice has become increasingly popular since the 1970s when Father Thomas Keating and others reintroduced it into the United States through the organization Contemplative Outreach.[1]

Centering prayer's roots reach back to the third century, when it was practiced widely by desert fathers and mothers—men and women who left the noise and chaos of the city to live in caves so they could seek wisdom and solitude. Saint Benedict also incorporated centering prayer as a daily practice for his monks to create a balanced rhythm of life.

The practice is simple. Here are the steps Casey suggested:

- Sit comfortably with your eyes closed and your head pointed downward so you can connect with your heart.
- Take a few deep breaths to relax your body.
- Choose a sacred word or phrase to hold in your heart (something simple such as *love*, *peace*, or *be still*).
- Silently speak the sacred word or phrase to yourself. Feel the words center themselves in your heart-space.
- When your mind drifts, return to the sacred word or phrase. Let the word or phrase become like a boat's anchor that stabilizes your mind and holds you securely in place.
- At the end of your meditation, sit in silence with eyes closed for a few more moments. Reflect on what you noticed or experienced.
- Then slowly open your eyes and move into your day.
- Return to your sacred word or phrase throughout the day to refocus and find your center again. You might even write the word on your to-do list or on a sticky note posted on your computer screen, mirror, or dashboard as a gentle reminder of what you experienced during your meditation practice.

"Wow! That sounds easy enough," I said to Casey. "Using a word or phrase to anchor my mind until it quiets itself sounds pretty doable. But what if it doesn't work? What if those noisy chimps still won't settle down?"

Imaginary Prayer

Casey said meditation is an awakening to—an awareness of—the presence of God within you. It's our personal encounter with Christ, an experience beyond words of the unique relationship between ourselves and the One who created us.

When we spend time with a loved one, we naturally develop a deeper relationship with them. We come to know them, discover their unique attributes and personality. We experience them.

It's the same with God, Casey said. As we spend time with the Creator in solitude, we learn more about him and ourselves. It's kind of like dating God first, then marrying him.

As the relationship grows, we learn more about who God is, and understand more of who we are. We discover the Creator is Love, someone who wishes to communicate with us, who desires to guide and lead us into wholeness. And we discover how to relate with each other. Uniquely. Divinely. Experientially.

Imaginary Prayer is a practice that invites us into that deeper experience and relationship with God and ourselves. Casey said Saint Ignatius taught it's okay to use our imaginations to draw deeper into God's Divine Love. It's why Jesus used parables to teach, so his followers could enter into the story and understand the lesson through their hearts instead of trying to figure it out in their minds.

Casey suggested trying this form of prayer by using the following process. At the beginning of your quiet time, open an inspirational book or Scripture and find a short story or parable you want to envision with your imagination.

For example, Casey said to read this verse from the Gospel of John: "One of his disciples—the one whom Jesus loved—was reclining next to him" (13:23).

Imagine you're the one Jesus loved dearly and you're leaning against him with your head on his shoulder. What does it feel like to rest on Jesus? What do you notice? What do you hear? What does your body feel like? What emotions do you experience?

Sit for as long as you like, imagining you are the Beloved. Notice if God says anything to you as you rest on Jesus's shoulder.

Then, ask yourself and the Creator, "What wisdom, what deeper understanding comes to me through this experience?"

Casey suggested keeping a journal to record my insights as I engage the spiritual practice of divine reading, or *lectio divina*. The entry for the day might be as simple as, "I am safe and loved." If you want, he said, you can go back and reread your journal from time to time. Let it become a living record of what you've discovered about yourself and the Source of Being.

I incorporated Casey's suggestions during my solitude the next morning. It helped a ton to quiet my monkey-mind.

Now when I enter solitude with the Creator each morning, I ask, "What do you want to do during our quiet time today?" Then I go with whatever practice feels life-giving.

And when the monkey-mind *ook! ooks!* at me, I give it something spiritually nourishing to chew on—a banana from God.

6

Can You Hear Me Now?

God Has a Voice. Can You Hear It?

"You look sad," Sandy commented as we left the parish council meeting. "Is there something wrong?"

I shrugged Sandy off. But she knew by my frown, something wasn't right in my world.

I fessed up. "Work's overwhelming. I've got an employee who keeps showing up late, calling in sick, and cat-clawing with other staff. I'm tired of dealing with other people's messiness. I don't know whether to fire her or give her a final written warning."

"Have you talked to God about it?"

My eyebrows crumpled as I glared back at Sandy. I'd never heard God's voice. I wasn't even sure he had one.

"I often hear God's voice," she matter-of-factly told me. "It's like a whisper. It has a unique tone. It's always the voice of love. I typically hear it when I'm quiet. Can you hear it too?"

Either Sandy was on drugs or she knew something I wanted to learn more about. Without waiting for a response, she told me something I'd never learned in religion class.

God's on the Phone

Hearing God's voice is a lot like the Verizon cell phone commercial where the guy's holding his phone to his ear in a rain forest and says, "Can you hear me *now*?" When the person on the other end of the line responds, "Yes," the Verizon man shouts, "*Good!*"

God's like the Verizon man, Sandy explained. He's always communicating with us. When we listen, hear the Divine Voice, and respond to it, the Great Communicator exclaims, "*Good!*"

"Imagine a personal dialogue with the Creator of the Universe." Sandy's voice softened as she pointed to my heart. "God wants to have a two-way conversation with us. He promises in Scripture, 'My sheep hear my voice and follow it'" (John 10:27).

Sandy said that God's always speaking to us and everyone can hear his voice. It's just that we haven't learned to recognize it or we're too busy doing all the talking and forget to take time to listen. Like any conversation with a loved one, we have to talk *and* listen. That creates space for two-way communication.

"Hearing from God is not a one-time event," Sandy continued. "It's not something we store in our dusty memories and refer to occasionally. Hearing from God is an ongoing conversation lived out daily. It becomes a lifestyle of listening."

Sandy told me the conversation with the Creator begins when we ask God to reveal to us what the Divine Voice sounds like. Then, like Samuel, who heard God whisper his name but recognized it was the Lord only after the third time, the more we open our hearts and practice fine-tuning our listening, we eventually become pretty good at recognizing God's voice.

God Conversations

The next day, I Googled the phrase "God's voice." I stumbled upon the online work of Tania Harris, an Australian pastor who leads God Conversations,[1] a global ministry that teaches people to recognize and respond to God's voice. Tania has an internet course called, "Heard from God Lately?"

I took the course, and over the next few weeks learned how talking and listening to God can become a normal part of our relationship with the Creator. Tania reminded me that the Creator of the Universe, the One who made the skies and stars, desires to communicate with us.

She says God is a talker. He spoke often throughout biblical history. He talked with Adam and Eve in the Garden. He conversed with Moses at the top of a smoky mountain. He told prophets about the future and gave revelations to the apostles. The phrase "and God said" appears so often in Scripture we almost overlook its significance.

On Pentecost, God went one step further. He poured the Holy Spirit into everyone's heart so we can experience and communicate with the Spirit directly.

Wow! I thought, as I pondered Tania's teachings. *Could it be possible God wants to communicate with me?*

What's God's Voice Sound Like?

I wondered, have I ever heard God's voice? If I did hear it, how would I know it's the Spirit's voice, not mine? Was it just wishful thinking to expect God would speak to me?

Put simply, I wanted to know what God's voice sounds like. So I looked for how others describe the Creator's voice.

Ridley Scott, in his epic movie *Exodus: Gods and Kings*, cast an eleven-year-old British schoolboy to play the role of the Spirit's voice. The director said the boy was chosen to exude innocence and purity.

In the movie *The Prince of Egypt*, each cast member whispered God's lines, so the Divine Voice sounded like a symphony of whispers.

In the Old Testament, Elijah experienced "sheer silence" he came to know as God's presence (1 Kgs 19:12).

I wondered, does God's voice sound like that of an innocent child? Does it sound like a whisper or a bunch of whispers at the same time? Is it deep and mature, like the voice of James Earl Jones? Is it gentle? Firm? Demanding? Does God have an accent?

Everything I discovered helped, but it didn't answer my basic question: "What does God's voice sound like?"

Ask and You'll Receive

I decided I'd follow Sandy's advice and ask the Creator to let me hear the Divine Voice. I figured I had nothing to lose. So, one day in my quiet time I put it out there. I asked the Spirit, "Would you teach me how to hear your voice?"

I didn't get an immediate response. But two months later at a week-long retreat put on by Casey and his Good News School of Lay Evangelization buddies, I was stunned when the Creator spoke powerfully to me.

During one of the morning teaching sessions, I got a peculiar notion that something bad was about to happen to my wife and children back home. The thought trembled like a volcano, spewing fear all over my insides. I shut my eyes and put my hand on my gut, hoping the wave of fright would pass. But it didn't. It got worse.

I figured it wasn't God's voice speaking to me; it was just my mind sputtering fear like it often does. The fear kept grabbing at my gut.

At the coffee break, I phoned my wife, but the call went into voicemail. Scared, I went into the empty church that stood next to the school. There I pleaded with God not to let anything bad happen to my family. I told God, "Take me. Take all of me. But don't take them."

Filled with angst, I fell prostrate on the floor and wept. Tears flooded my body like a second baptism.

After a few minutes, which seemed like hours, I stood up. Behind the altar was a huge crucifix. As I stared at it, I noticed it wasn't Jesus's body on the cross; it was mine. Like Moses at the burning bush, it was like I was in some kind of a mystical experience. Surrendering.

And then I heard an inner voice. It was soft and gentle like air flowing through a flute on the inside of my chest. It was loving and kind. It whispered, "I love you. I wouldn't take them from you. All is well." I knew in that moment it was God's voice I heard.

Joy melted my fear. I ran outside, pulled out my cell phone, and called my wife. She confirmed all was well. She and our children were fine.

God's Voice Is Unique

The memory of that soft whisper I experienced that day etched itself in my heart. I believe that experience was the answer to my prayer asking to hear God's voice.

Since then, whenever I hear that whisper—when I experience that gentle air flowing between my heart and stomach, feel the silent stream of love caressing the inside of my lungs, notice the calming presence in my body, or melt with tears that soothe my soul—I've come to trust it's the voice of God.

Mother Teresa says the language of God is silence. By

creating space to be quiet and listen, the whisper of the Holy Spirit eventually comes upon us.[2]

Entering into Presence

Paul Smith, a retired pastor and teacher, in his article "Discovering Your Divine Voice," has this to say about discovering the voice of God:

> To begin listening, first become aware of the presence of Jesus or other saintly guidance. This moves us to a subtle state of consciousness which is filled with information and spiritual energy and presences. When God speaks to us internally, it is through the thoughts, images, or intuitions that come to our mind while we are in a receptive state. In time we learn the quality of this state of consciousness. The Bible calls it the presence of the holy spirit.
>
> Then wait quietly for the first thought or image that arises. Don't try to figure something out. Is it a reasonable, sensible thought? Or is it wild and strange? The truth is, God can speak in any of those voices! Only experimenting and gaining experience will gradually help you be comfortable with knowing what to pay attention to. We don't always get it right, and that's why [Saint] Paul offered the safety net of others discerning how helpful it is.
>
> With experience we can begin to sense the slight difference between our normal inner monologue and our deep, divine Self. Whatever comes from deep within us comes with a hint of flow and a slight boldness. It's still us, but it's the deep us.[3]

God's Voice Is Often Our Voice

Smith says that because we're created in God's image and likeness and are one with him, the Divine Voice can often sound like our own voice. Wouldn't it be just like God to blend the Divine Voice with our human voice because it's familiar to us? Smith writes,

> So, whenever we are listening inwardly for what God is creating with us for others, God *intends it* be a divine mixture of us and God. Words, images, and intuitions from God sound like us because they partly are! God so cleverly blends God's Divine Nature with our Divine Nature (True Self) that we can't really tell the difference between them. That's called Oneness—"I pray that they may be one as you Abba and I are one." We can now participate in the divine nature of God![4]

The Still, Small Voice

At that parish council meeting years ago, Sandy introduced me to the concept of God's voice and our ability to hear it. It opened a door to experiencing God like never before. Now when I have a problem, I take it to the Creator during quiet time and ask for guidance. The solution often comes to me in a still, small voice within my heart.

I've come to believe Sandy was one of God's human messengers. Her words were a nudge to begin searching for the Divine Voice speaking within me.

Maybe the words on this page feel like a nudge to you too. If you desire to experience God's voice as a guiding force in your life, just ask the Spirit to let you hear that Voice. Then listen with the ears of your heart. Let the Creator surprise you.

"Can you hear me *now*?" God might say.

If and when you do, give the Creator a high-five as you both exclaim, "*Good!*"

7

What's a God-Nudge?
Do the Holy-Pokey with the Creator

I was having coffee one day with Mary, a good friend and spiritual director (she's taken a bunch of classes to learn about discernment and hearing God's voice, and all that great stuff). I was telling her how I was feeling overwhelmed by life: four kids, a demanding job, a big mortgage, and all the other responsibilities an adult has to juggle—it was all squashing the joy out of me.

I told Mary I believed in God. It's just the Creator felt distant. I felt my problems weren't important to the Keeper of the Universe. God has more important things to deal with, like protecting the environment, stopping people from killing each other—you know, the weighty matters. Why would God care about me and my petty issues?

"I wish I could experience God directly, face-to-face, like the relationship I have with my wife, family, and friends," I lamented. "I get to see them every day, interact with them, and sometimes get their advice about a situation troubling me. And we have lots of fun together."

God-Hotline

After taking another sip of coffee, I stroked my chin and pondered out loud, "If I were God, I'd give everybody a cell

44

phone they could use to dial up and talk with me. We'd each get a direct-dial number for the Creator. Whenever we felt sad or lonely, we'd type in our magic phone number and the Creator would remind us we're loved unconditionally. When we needed instructions on how to deal with a tough situation, we'd be able to dial the God-Hotline and get some Divine Wisdom. If God was busy talking with someone else, it'd be fine if there was a prerecorded message for the standard questions like, Why did you create me? Am I good? Am I going to heaven?" At least we'd be able to hear the voice of our loving Father.

Mary said that God doesn't work that way. Instead, God works through the ordinary people and events in our lives. The Creator placed the Holy Spirit in our hearts, and if we get quiet, sit patiently, and listen each day, we can learn the distinct sound of God's whisper.

According to Mary, God wants what's best for us, so he's always inviting us toward deeper love and wholeness. It's our job to learn how to see what she calls the "God-nudges" in our lives and follow them.

I leaned forward and asked Mary to explain.

Nudges Come in All Shapes

"Nudges come in all shapes and sizes," she said. "There's the jab in the ribs from a co-worker at a meeting with your boss, prodding you to speak up and ask for the raise you've been wanting. There's the 'I love you, man' fist bump from your buddy when he greets you. And the kick to your shins when your spouse is trying to tell you you're sharing too much information with your children about some of the crazy things you did in college. Nudges convey messages. Each poke carries instruction, correction, or guidance as we go about our ordinary lives. When we listen to the nudges and follow their lead, they become extraordinary because we see the wisdom in them. They become guideposts on our life's journeys."

God-Nudges

Mary said the Creator nudges us too. She calls them "God-nudges" because they're usually about a choice or a direction we're being invited to take in life. They typically come in questions or coincidences that prod us to move or grow.

To figure out how God has been guiding me during my life, Mary suggested I make a timeline and identify each of the God-nudges in my life. According to Mary, when we look in the rearview mirror of our lives, we discover how we've grown over time—on the inside. We connect the dots to gain deeper understanding about ourselves and God's movement in our lives. In doing so, we sharpen our ability to recognize the God-nudges poking us.

Looking Back to Grow Forward

Mary suggested I divide my life into decades. For each decade, she told me to pinpoint where I'd experienced God's loving guidance.

It seemed like a great idea, a way to figure out what God had been up to in my life through its ups and downs. Who knows, maybe I'd even gain some wisdom!

So, one morning, I took a sheet of newsprint paper, spread it onto the floor, and drew a long horizontal line on it. Then I put vertical lines on the paper dividing my life into decades: ages 1–10, 11–20, 21–30, and so on. That was the easy part.

I sat back, took a long look at each decade, and pondered. Then I pondered some more. Nothing jumped out at me. My mind raced with those *this-is-stupid* thoughts like it often does.

Refusing to give up, I asked the Creator for some help. Help me pinpoint your nudges in my life for each decade, I prayed.

"I thought you'd never ask." I heard a silent chuckle from God.

It wasn't an audible sound. It might have been just my imagination or my own voice I heard. But somehow when I asked the Creator to help me, the memories flowed. Slowly, decade by decade, the mile markers, game-changers, and life experiences that shaped and molded me became evident.

Life in the Ditches

The most significant God-nudge I discovered happened at age eighteen during my senior year of high school.

Back then, I was trying to figure out what I was supposed to do with my life. My dad had died of cancer a year earlier. I felt lost and confused. I struggled to decide whether to become a priest or a lawyer.

One night, at a weekend vocation retreat at the Oblates of Mary Immaculate Center in Washington, D.C., I knelt on clumsy teenager knees gazing for hours out the window of my room, staring at the gold cross atop the Basilica of the National Shrine of the Immaculate Conception. I asked God to help me understand what he wanted me to do with the rest of my life. I had no idea at age eighteen how to listen to God's voice. I didn't even know he had a voice. I had never heard of the word *discernment*.

So, I just went with my gut that night as I looked up at the cross and the stars. I told God I couldn't become a priest because the celibacy thing was too hard.

I wanted to get married and have a family. I wanted to dig in the ditches in the workaday world, supporting my wife and kids. I wanted to see how God would keep me safe and faithful to him in the business world where people shove and push, the disjointed family world where siblings don't always get along with each other, in the divine chaos world of raising a family, where the love and laughter of children restores joy to your tired heart.

These thoughts became a guidepost. So, I put them into words, as well as I could, on my timeline.

That's the Good Stuff

Next, I marked on the timeline all the good stuff in my life.

I've been gifted with a beautiful wife who's been my soulmate for the past thirty-seven years. I'm blessed with four healthy, strong children successfully growing into young adulthood. And I've been privileged to own my own law firm and work as an attorney in a busy law practice for over a quarter century of my life.

And the Tough Stuff

But like everyone else, the journey's not been without struggle. So, I also put on my timeline the bout with depression in my thirties that nudged me into joining a twelve-step group to work through the death of my father. I marked how my perfectionism had become an enemy, resulting in seeking counseling to learn how to deal with anxiety.

As I completed my timeline, I stepped back and realized that many of my life's experiences were in fact God-nudges. And when I responded to them positively, even stumbled through them, the Creator guided me with love and wisdom along life in the ditches.

Do the Holy-Pokey

I'm pretty sure we all experience God-nudges in our lives. Mary had them when the angel asked her if she would carry the Son of God in her womb. Joseph got nudged through a dream that told him not to divorce Mary. Mother Teresa felt the holy poke when she realized she was being called to change her vocation as a private school teacher and minister to those at death's doorstep.

God-nudges sometimes come in small ways—should I read this book, take this class, join a church, or seek guidance from a spiritual mentor?

They also come in big ways—what am I to do with the rest of my life?

If we listen and ask for clarity, God-nudges become part of life's dance. They're like doing the holy-pokey with the Creator.

Part Two

SPIRITUAL READING

Just as food is necessary to the life of the body, so good reading is necessary to the life of the soul.

—Pope John XXIII

8

Gimme Thirty!
Take Thirty Minutes Each Day for Spiritual Reading

"How about you set aside thirty minutes each day for spiritual reading?" Don prodded.

Don's the mentor I meet with once a month to reflect on how my spiritual life's going. I nicknamed him "Eagle Don" because he has intense eyes and probably hangs out with God, gliding around the clouds, then swooping down to impart wisdom.

"Seriously? Do you know how busy my life is?" I replied. "Between four kids, my wife, a demanding career as a lawyer, and chores around the house, you want me to squeeze in one more thing?"

"You go to the gym daily to exercise your body, don't you?" Don asked.

"Yep," I said, waiting for Don to swoop down with timeless wisdom.

Don explained that just as working out at the gym is necessary to maintain healthy bodies, inspirational reading is necessary to maintain healthy souls. It gives new insights, helps us make sense of ourselves and the world. It provides wisdom to chew on throughout the day.

My workout buddy Ben said something similar a few weeks before my meeting with Don. Ben's one of the most disciplined people I know. He creates an annual vision plan for his business and sets personal goals to nurture his mind, body, and spirit. He then writes his vision plan on a white board in his office so he can see it each day and make his dreams become a reality.

One of the top items on Ben's vision board is to spend at least thirty minutes each day reading a chapter from a good book. Ben told me he goes upstairs to his bedroom a half-hour early each night. He sits in bed and reads.

I didn't pay any attention to Ben when he told me about his daily reading habit. I figured he was just an over-the-top Type-A personality. But when Don suggested the same thing, I figured it was a God-nudge, and I needed to pay attention.

This Is How We Grow

Spiritual writer Reena Mathur says inspirational reading is a vital part of human growth.[1] It deepens our knowledge and makes us a better person. If you've ever met someone full of life, positivity, and happiness, she says, it's a good bet that person has a habit of reading. Reading a good book has the power to lift your mood and bring a smile to your face.

Mathur notes these benefits from spiritual reading:

- **Lowered stress levels.** Reading spiritual books improves your mental and physical health. Studies have proven that people who read are more likely to stay calm in stressful situations.
- **Enhanced power, concentration, and focus.** Reading enhances your focus and concentration

levels. The words within spiritual books offer
constructive ways to empower you.

- **New perspectives.** Inspirational books expand
your thinking and sharpen your imagination.
They shower divine light and wisdom upon you.
- **Deeper truths.** The Bible and other inspirational books teach us deeper truths about life.
They define the value and importance of our
human souls. They help us understand ourselves, the world, and all Creation.

According to spiritual writer Susan M. Erschen, "The
more we can open ourselves to a wide variety of spiritual writing, the more we will hear God speaking in our lives." Erschen
writes,

Spiritual reading can offer us a smorgasbord of
messages. Words of courage for when we are afraid.
Words of peace for when we are angry. Words of joy
for when we are sad. Words of faith for when we
have doubts. Spiritual reading can make sense of
things we never understood before. It can open our
eyes to our faith in ways we never considered.[2]

Erschen says spiritual reading is like a treasure hunt. We
search for words to comfort and inspire us. We explore new
thoughts and ideas that lead us up "new mountains or guide
us through unexpected dark valleys." She offers these tips to
get the most out of spiritual reading:

- Schedule a regular daily reading time.
- Sign up for several daily meditations and reflec-
tions to get in your email each morning.

- When you find a word or phrase that inspires you, write it down and put it someplace where you can see and enjoy it repeatedly.
- Replace some of your television or social media time with spiritual reading. Keep the spiritual books you're reading in a handy place so you can easily pick them up when you have down time.
- Journal about what you're learning from your reading so you can integrate it into your daily life.

Reading Shapes and Empowers Us

As I pondered what Don, Ben, Mathur, and Erschen said, I got to thinking about Jesus and how he was always reading during his time on earth. He unrolled the scrolls in the temple and studied and memorized the words of the Old Testament. He integrated what he read into his life. The words shaped and formed him, helped him understand his life's purpose. They became words he quoted for strength and courage.

At his baptism, Jesus heard the Old Testament words from Psalm 2:7, "You are my son," and Isaiah 42:1, "Here is my servant...my chosen, in whom my soul delights; I have put my spirit upon him; he will bring forth justice to the nations." These words clarified Jesus's calling. They inspired him to claim the truth of God's divine plan for him.

As he hung on the cross, Jesus cried out the words of Psalm 22, "My God, my God, why have you forsaken me?" And at the moment of his death, Jesus quoted Psalm 31:5, "Into your hand I commit my spirit; you have redeemed me, O Lord, faithful God."

He must have read and memorized those words repeatedly during his thirty-three years on earth. They weren't merely words on a scroll; they were words that empowered him as he integrated what he read into his life.

A Life-Giving Habit

I figured it was probably a good idea to follow Jesus's example. So I put Don and Ben's suggestion into practice. I asked God to give me the gentle discipline to go to bed a half-hour earlier each night and lead me to a book that would inspire me to grow.

At 8:30 that night (I'm not much of a night owl), I stood in my den looking at my bookshelves pondering which book to pick. Henri Nouwen's *Return of the Prodigal Son* leapt out, calling, "Read me!" I pulled the book off the shelf, headed up to bed, and read for the next thirty minutes.

The words in Nouwen's book spoke like they'd been FedExed overnight to my doorstep:

> I am the prodigal son every time I search for uncon-
> ditional love where it cannot be found. Why do I
> keep ignoring the place of true love and persist in
> looking for it elsewhere? Why do I keep leaving
> home where I am called a child of God, the Beloved
> of my Father?[3]

Tears rolled down my cheeks as the words flowed gently into my soul: I am God's Beloved, I pondered. He loves me just the way I am.

I've often struggled with self-worth, and Nouwen's words were the balm my soul needed. It was as if God handpicked that book to tuck me into bed that night. As I continued reading over the next several weeks, a shift occurred in me. The old tapes in my head that blared, "You're bad. Messed up. An embarrassment," quieted. They were replaced with the words, "You are my Beloved upon whom my favor rests." Throughout the days, I often savor those words as God continues to shape and mold me with them.

Give yourself a treat—the gift of a daily "Gimme thirty!" It's the spiritual food that feeds and empowers our souls.

9

Get the Funk Out
Finding God in the Bookstore

I continued my nightly reading ritual for several weeks. But like many good intentions that fall by the wayside, after I'd finished Nouwen's book, I fell off the reading wagon.

I didn't notice the shift in me at first. But as the old tapes blared their familiar "you're no good!" refrains in my head, I knew something was out of balance, but I couldn't pinpoint what.

I met with Don for spiritual direction the next month and brought my lament to him.

"I'm stuck in a funk. I feel numb, like I'm ghosting through life again. Drifting. Overwhelmed," I complained.

"What's the funk telling you?" he replied. "What would be life-giving?"

"I need something to chew on, jump-start me, get me out of my head, and back into my heart."

"Here's an idea. How about you look for God in the book-store?"

"What?"

Don explained that when we're feeling anxious, irritable, or out of sorts, it's often a sign God's inviting us to push gently against the negative thoughts and emotions by doing something that will help us grow. He said Saint Ignatius of Loyola calls this shifting pattern of spiritual growth *consolation* and *desolation*.

Are You in Consolation or Desolation?

Consolation occurs when we feel connected to ourselves and God—when our days are filled with joy, blessing, and gratitude. We're in consolation when we have faith, hope, and love. We have a sense of God's closeness. Peace and tranquility fill our hearts.

When we experience consolation, Ignatius says keep doing what you're doing because your inner work is paying off. You're in tune with the Holy Spirit and receiving the Spirit's gifts. You're in the *flow*.

Desolation rears its head when we experience disorder—when we feel disconnected from God and ourselves. We're in desolation when we lack faith, hope, and love. God feels distant. We're restless, agitated, filled with fear and worry. We isolate as we try to hide from ourselves and others.

When desolation occurs, Ignatius says go back and pinpoint when it started. Then push gently against it by doing something different, like increasing your quiet time or finding a book that will help you understand how to move into consolation.

Don told me Ignatius came up with these concepts after having been struck by a cannonball during a fierce battle. Hospitalized, bored, and bedridden for months, Ignatius stumbled upon the only two books in the hospital library: one about the lives of the saints and the other about Christ's life.

What's Discernment? How Do You Do It?

Both books inspired Ignatius. He studied more and wrote extensively about the gift of discernment—the ability to discover where and how God's guiding us in our lives. Ignatius is the go-to guy for learning about discernment. In the 1500s, he wrote the book *The Spiritual Exercises of St. Ignatius*, which is a compilation of prayers, meditations, and spiritual practices to help us discover the movement of the Holy Spirit.

Sitting with Don, I recalled when my desolation had started. "That's it," I said as a smile cracked the frown on my face. "The gang of noisy head-bangers returned when I stopped my daily reading."

"Exactly. You slipped into desolation. You stopped nourishing your soul with wisdom."

Don told me to push against the funk that overshadowed me by heading to a physical or online bookstore and asking God to lead me to a book that would speak to my heart.

"Wander through the bookstore aisles and pray for a book to leap off the shelf. Pull the books out one at a time. Read their titles. Look at their table of contents and back covers. Ask God if this is the right one for you. When you feel that take-me-home-and-read-me twang in your belly, trust God's handing the book to you."

The next day, I headed to the bookstore. Glancing up and down the aisles of books lining the spirituality section, I shook my head, scrunched my nose, and wondered if I'd ever find what I was looking for. Then I remembered what Don suggested about asking God to point me to a book. And so, I did. Right in Walden's Bookstore, I made the sign of the cross and asked the Creator to drop a book on me.

After a half hour of reaching and pulling, picking up one book after another and shoving them back onto the shelf when they didn't hit the sweet spot, one book jumped out at me: *God's Voice Within—The Ignatian Way to Discover God's Will* by Mark E. Thibodeaux, SJ.[1] It was all about discernment—listening to the Spirit's movement in our thoughts, emotions, and bodily reactions, and then using that information to make wise, life-giving choices in all aspects of our lives.

"*Discernment.* That's what God's inviting me to!" I exclaimed aloud as the lady standing next to me gave me a side-eye look that screamed, *Shush!*

As I opened Thibodeaux's book and scanned its table of contents, I realized the Creator wanted to teach me how to listen to his inner voice and let it guide me. Dropping my spiritual reading had led me down the path of frustration and anxiety. God was calling me back to consolation through the daily practice of giving him thirty minutes each day to speak through the inspired words of others—words that spring from the wisdom of God.

I began reading Thibodeaux's book that night. It was like God was sending love letters through the words on the pages, teaching me how to hear his inner voice and discover the tools of discernment.

In *God's Voice Within*, Thibodeaux writes, "Ignatius was not so much interested in creating a foolproof, step-by-step manual for decision-making but wanted to shape the kind of person who could intuitively sense the spirits of the movements within her and thereby could know God's will. Ignatius was interested in building not a *process* of discernment but rather a *person* of discernment. Once a person has developed this Ignatian intuition, discernment will flow more naturally and smoothly."[2]

Thibodeaux's words taught me there's no cookbook recipe for how to discern God's loving movement in our lives.

Instead, we can follow this general framework to make wise, discerning choices:

- **Get quiet.** To hear God's voice, we have to turn down the noise of the world by creating a consistent daily time for sitting quietly and listening for the whisper of the Holy Spirit.
- **Look at options and gather data.** Write down and evaluate the options available and research the information needed to make an informed choice. You can even make a pros and cons list for each option to see which ones outweigh the others.
- **Dream dreams.** God dwells within the deepest desires of our hearts. It's his primary way of communicating with us. Let God dream in and with you. Ask, "What would be life-giving for me and others?"
- **Ponder the dreams.** "Praydream." Through your imagination, live out each option available, asking which one brings joy, excitement, and deeper consolation for you.

By talking it out with Don, I realized my funk was an invitation to push against the desolation I was encountering. I've gotten back onto the spiritual reading wagon that's so vital for the soul.

Whenever the noisy head-bangers take up space in my head again, I know it's a sign to head to the bookstore and find a new book that speaks to my heart. It's a good way to get the funk out.

10

Find True North

Gather Your Friends and Chew on Life's Wisdom

"I've been diagnosed with cancer," Tom told us. His jaw stiffened. "I'm scared. I don't know where this journey will take me. I'd appreciate it if you could hold me in prayer and go into silence for a few moments. Be present to God for me. Help me hear what the Spirit is trying to say."

Tom's part of our Inner Compass Group—a group of five guys who get together once a month for either group spiritual direction or a book discussion. We call it an Inner Compass Group, or ICG for short, because the Holy Spirit is the inner compass that guides us like a magnetic gizmo used to find direction when lost in the woods. Our Divine Compass points us to the heart's True North. It helps us discover the wisdom the Spirit offers on the path toward wholeness.

Tom took a few more minutes to share his fears and concerns. We then went into silence, held him in prayer, and listened for what the Holy Spirit placed upon our hearts.

After several moments, we offered what we'd heard in the quiet for Tom.

"I heard these words from Scripture: 'I am with you always. Do not be afraid,'" Steve said.

Ralph spoke next. "The image that rose up in me was that of John laying his head upon Jesus's chest at the last supper. You were John and Jesus was holding you."

"The song, 'Be Not Afraid,' rose up in me as I lifted you in prayer," Peter said.

After each of us offered what the Spirit had placed on our hearts, Tom's eyes shined with glimmers of hope.

"Guys, I can't thank you enough for holding me in prayer. I admit the fear of the unknown overwhelms me. But your words and images give me strength. I think God's telling me he's walking alongside me. He's got this. I'm safe in his arms."

The Wisdom of Group Spiritual Direction

Our ICG group follows a simple and practical process outlined by Rose Mary Dougherty, SSND, in her book *Group Spiritual Direction—Community for Discernment.* Rose Mary writes,

> Group spiritual direction is grounded in Mystery. We use a very simple process which honors and supports this grounding: silence, the sharing of a participant, silence, response from the group, silence. We repeat this process until all individuals have had a time for their sharing and response from the group.[1]

Following her outline, when our ICG group gathers, the facilitator starts the meeting with a short reflection. He invites us to let go of the day and be present to God's Spirit.

The facilitator then asks one of us to share what we've brought to the group to hold in prayer. We listen, hold the person in silence, and respond with what we heard in our hearts.

This simple format provides a safe space to get into the nitty-gritty of our lives. We break the "man code"—those unwritten rules that say men can only share superficially about things like work, sports, and cars. The man code says men are sissies if they get vulnerable and share their fears and faith journeys. ICG groups—whether made up of men or a combination of men and women—unlock the doors of our lives so we can chew on wisdom and learn from others.

Throughout the five years we've been meeting, our group has dug deep and shared intimate stories as we seek wisdom and direction from God. One of the guy's talked about the immense suffering he experienced after his wife's suicide; another asked for help making a career decision to leave the marketplace and become a full-time artist; and another shared his joy at the birth of his first grandchild.

Shaking It Up

"I love our ICG group, but I'm getting tired of talking about the same old things," Ralph complained at one meeting. "I don't feel like we're growing. It's time to dive deeper. What if we shake it up with some spiritual book discussions sometimes."

"Great idea!" Rik responded. "How about we read Richard Hauser's *Moving in the Spirit*[2] for next month's Inner Compass Group? I'll send out some questions we can discuss when we get together next month."

The guys accepted Rik's offer as we dug into reading Hauser's book. Little did I know my perspective about God was about to be reshaped.

Who's in Control Here?

Hauser states there are two models for our relationship with the Creator. One's the correct one; the other, flat out wrong. One model suggests: We initiate—God rewards. The other states: God initiates—we respond.[3]

Hauser calls the first model the Western model. It's the pattern most of us follow.

The Western model suggests we're in control. When we do good, God rewards us. We initiate the relationship by striving to be perfect, and when we act right, God's supposed to respond by giving us what we desire—wealth, good health, a happy family.

As I read Hauser's explanation, it reminded me of Pinocchio. We pretend we're Geppetto and God's Pinocchio. We try to pull God's strings by doing good stuff and expect God will then shower us with blessing. We think we're in control, but we're really not, because we're always seeking to please God and gain the Creator's favor. It eventually becomes exhausting when even as we do good, bad things happen.

During our book discussion, I shared with the ICG group that this model was the one I followed growing up. When I wanted something from God or felt like I'd messed up, I'd go to daily Mass for weeks or say a fifty-four-day rosary novena.

While going to Mass and saying the rosary are good things, they didn't improve my relationship with God. If I didn't get what I wanted, I figured the Big Guy was angry with me and giving me the silent treatment. If I broke the fifty-four-day rosary novena, I decided I was a loser and my slacker attitude had shut down the grace pipeline.

So, I'd either step up my holy-moly practices or give up on God and walk away because he wasn't giving me what I wanted. He wasn't being a team player.

The guys helped me understand the Western model was wrong because I wasn't listening to God. I was trying to pull his strings. I was trying to earn God's favor by being the perfect altar boy, even as an adult.

But God's not a puppet-god. And hard as I might try, I'm never going to reach perfection.

With my friends' help and Hauser's inspiration, I realized it was time to let go of the false beliefs I'd developed. It was time to discover who God *really* is.

The In-To-Me-See God

The second model is the scriptural one, according to Hauser. It's consistent with how the Bible describes our relationship with God.

It suggests God is always initiating and moving in our lives, his Divine love drawing us closer toward wholeness, inner peace, and balance. Our job is to listen and determine where and how God's guiding us, and then respond by following the Spirit's lead.

The scriptural model reminds us we're God's Beloved. The Creator is the One who made us and wants what's best for us. Because we're unconditionally loved by our Creator, we've been gifted with discernment—the Spirit within us that invites us to listen to God's voice and follow his loving nudges.

Hauser describes discernment as "my effort with God's grace to respond always to the movement of the Spirit within myself."[4] The word comes from the French root *discerner—to separate by sifting; to distinguish between; to perceive; to learn wisdom.*[5]

Dave, one of the ICG guys, said he likes to think of his relationship with God as one of intimacy. Dave defines *intimacy* as "in-to-me-see." He says, "When I trust God, know he's got my back, and wants me to be happy, I let God see my innermost self. I open my heart and let him see-into-me."

As I listened to Dave describe his relationship with God, I yearned to know the God Dave knew.

"It's a two-way street," Dave continued. "As I let God see into me, he lets me see into him. He lets me know his heart overflows with love for me. He'd do anything for me. He talks to me in whispers. When I need affirmation, he's there with a Presence I can't fully describe—but I know is real. And most important, when I need direction, unlike a human compass that points to the magnetic north pole and can be off, he guides me with my Inner Compass to True North—the divine path on which I'm traveling."

After reading Hauser's book and discussing it with the ICG group, I came to understand there's a hidden Presence within each of us that constantly works to bring us into deeper intimacy (in-to-me-see) with God—to bring about good in our lives because God wants us to be happy.

This hidden Presence is the Holy Spirit. The more we learn about him, the more we can respond to his guidance in our lives. By listening for "God-nudges" we can recognize the Spirit's movement in our lives. And since the language of God is silence, when we listen with our hearts, we strengthen the spiritual muscle of discernment. We respond to the inner movement of the Holy Spirit.

Reading Hauser's book with my ICG buddies unlocked a key to one of life's mysteries. I realized my perspective about God was all wrong. Because of Hauser's wisdom, I've stopped trying to be a perfect altar boy—the adult kid trying to please

Daddy—and instead, set aside daily quiet time to stop and listen for Divine directions.

Whether it's a book study or a group spiritual direction gathering, when we join together each month, we create space for God. We give each other the gift of being present to the Creator. In a multitude of ways, the Spirit shows up with what each one of us needs. Together we chew on life's wisdom and find True North.

Part Three

COMMUNITY

community

We are called to be strong companions and clear mirrors to one another, to seek those who reflect with compassion and a keen eye how we are doing, whether we seem centered or off course....We need the nourishing company of others to create the circle needed for growth, freedom, and healing.

—Wayne Muller

11

Who's in Your Spiritual Tribe?

Consider the Gift of Spiritual Direction

Did you ever notice how writers, public speakers, and other ten-steps-to-happiness gurus come up with all sorts of recommendations for your life but don't give you the recipe to find what they say you need?

Take, for example, the popular catchphrase, "find your tribe." Jane Howard, in her book *Families*, tells me I need one. "Call it a clan, call it a network, call it a tribe, call it a family. Whatever you call it, whoever you are, you need one."[1]

Great advice, but Howard doesn't tell me how to *find* a tribe. Do I post a yard sign in my front lawn saying, "Looking for a tribe," hoping someone will knock on my door? Do I put a post on Facebook telling the world I need to find a tribe and expect someone will shoot me an instant message and claim me as part of their tribe?

I don't think it works that way—at least it hasn't for me.

Who's in Your
Inner Circle of Trust?

At the retreat I attended with Casey-the-lay-evangelist, he told me finding your *spiritual* tribe differs from finding a few good friends to hang out with. "If we want to grow spiritually," he said, "we need to surround ourselves with a community of like-minded people to inspire, nudge, and help us discover who we are and how we're being invited by the Holy Spirit to grow."

Unfortunately, there's no how-to manual on finding your tribe. It's all about listening and letting the Spirit guide us, and then being intentional about who we place in our inner circle of trust.

Our spouses, partners, friends, church community, and family are all important members of our tribe because they help teach and shape us as we live and work with them.

But Casey said we also need teachers and mentors as part of our tribe—people one step farther than us along the spiritual path who shine the flashlight of wisdom on our trail. One teacher is a spiritual director, a person trained in the art of discernment who listens and helps us gain clarity about where the Holy Spirit is guiding us.

When Casey suggested I find a spiritual director— something I'd never heard about—I asked him if I could just Google the term *spiritual gurus* or look up *palm readers* in the classified ads and find one? Casey rolled his eyes and shook his head. It was clear I wasn't much interested in finding a spiritual director, just then. Several years later, spiritual direction bumped into me.

Here's what happened.

Bumping into Spiritual Direction

"Honey, I'm selling the house. I've discovered a loophole. If I become an Episcopalian minister, I can sneak back into the Catholic Church as a married priest," I announced to my wife after returning from a week-long retreat at a monastery.

Denise, my wife, folded her arms across her chest, rolled her eyeballs with an "*Oh, brother, here goes another Don Quixote adventure*" look, and replied, "That's pretty big stuff. Don't you think you should talk with someone about it—like Joanne."

Joanne's the director of religious education at the church we attend. As I considered my wife's suggestion, I figured I could meet with Joanne and convince her my idea was totally God-inspired. With Joanne's help, we'd be able to persuade Denise she needed to surrender to what I'm sure an angel whispered to me at the retreat one morning, as I sat trying to figure out what I was supposed to do with the second half of my middle-aged life.

Spiritual Direction Nudges

I called and scheduled an appointment with Joanne. The next afternoon as I sat in her office and explained what the angel told me, she suggested I meet with a spiritual director.

"What's that?" I asked.

Joanne pulled up the definition of *spiritual direction* from the website of the Spiritual Life Center in West Hartford, Connecticut. She read it aloud:

> Spiritual Direction, also known [as] Spiritual Companionship, is a process of deepening a person's spirituality. Spirituality is the term used to describe every person's response to and relationship with

75

the Sacred (God, The Divine, The Holy, The Spirit) as the Sacred is experienced in one's life. Spirituality can be as intimate as the deepest emotions and relationships and as wide and diverse as the cosmos.[2]

I still wasn't sure about this spiritual direction stuff. I imagined someone looking into a crystal ball, like the fortune-teller Dorothy consulted in that dingy trailer in the *Wizard of Oz*, or someone chain-smoking cigarettes while reading tarot cards. Joanne told me I had the wrong idea.

A Short History of Spiritual Direction

According to Joanne, the practice of spiritual direction dates back to the third century with the desert fathers and mothers. In those days, men and women left the city and traveled into the desert to meet with hermits who'd devoted their lives to full-time prayer and devotion to God. The "city folk," as Joanne called them, would go to the desert fathers or mothers and ask for spiritual guidance. Then the city folk returned to their daily lives. They came back to the desert regularly to meet with their mentors to seek ongoing guidance.

As the church developed, spiritual direction moved into the sacrament of confession for laypeople. The focus of spiritual direction then shifted toward developing priests, brothers, and nuns into more orthodox and faithful leaders.

But spiritual direction made a resurgence in the mid-twentieth century, when the Second Vatican Council encouraged all people—including the laity—to return to the ancient practice of spiritual direction.

Joanne showed me an article by Russell Shaw titled "Why Not Spiritual Direction?"[3] In the article, Shaw points out that in 1988, Pope John Paul II in *Christifideles Laici* reemphasized spiritual direction as a necessary element in the formation of laypeople.[4]

Hmmm...I pondered. It didn't sound like Joanne wanted to get onboard with my idea of convincing my wife that I was supposed to become an Episcopalian priest. Sitting in Joanne's office, I scratched the back of my neck and scrunched my face.

Okay, I thought. Maybe it wasn't an angel that told me to leave the Catholic Church and become an Episcopalian minister. Maybe I just discovered the loophole in one of the canon law books I read when I was in the library at the retreat house. Maybe my lawyer brain had mistakenly convinced myself I'd experienced a God-nudge.

The confused look on my face told Joanne I needed more convincing. She gave me a copy of an article titled "10 Reasons to Get a Spiritual Director."[5]

In it, spiritual mentor Larissa Marks outlines the focus of spiritual direction:

1. Explore and interpret your experiences of God.
2. Integrate spirituality and practices in your daily life.
3. Deepen your relationship with God.
4. Make important decisions or changes.
5. Discover your purpose and calling in life.
6. Share joys, fears, desires, and struggles in a safe environment.
7. Spiritually heal from past wounds and hurts.
8. Receive the encouragement, guidance, and companionship you need.
9. Get spiritually unstuck.
10. Become who you were designed to be.

After reading the article, I agreed with Joanne I probably didn't hear an angel. Instead, God was nudging, and I was stumbling into spiritual direction.

Like a blind man who'd been given his first glimpse of light, I said, "Okay. Let's do it." I asked Joanne to point me to a spiritual director who might be a good fit.

The next week I met Charm.

Looking Through Our God-Lens

Standing in the hallway, I peered into the spiritual direction room. It was about the size of a large walk-in closet. There was a lamp, coffee table, three chairs, and a cross on the wall.

The chairs were old and worn, the kind you'd see in your grandmother's house, the kind you knew a lot of people had sat in before, drinking water or coffee, conversing about God and life. The room was still warm with their lingering presence.

Charm was sitting in one chair with an open book in her lap. I sensed she was in prayer. She was an older woman with gray hair and wire-rimmed glasses. I guessed she was around seventy. I later learned she'd been a spiritual director for over thirty years.

I knocked on the open door. Charm stood up and greeted me with a warm smile.

"It's nice to meet you, brian," Charm said. "I've been holding you in prayer since Joanne contacted me. I'm looking forward to walking alongside you on your spiritual path. Please, sit down."

After introductions, Charm and I talked about my faith life. I told her about the retreat and my mistake about the angel. I told her I'd been raised believing in God, and still did believe, but my life had gotten so full of lots of good but demanding stuff that I wasn't sure who God was anymore. I wasn't sure who I was.

I straightened in the chair, cleared my throat, and tried to hold back my tears. Charm's eyes pierced through to my soul.

"Honey, you're in the desert," she offered, leaning forward to reach out and hold my hands. "Deserts are scary places. But they're also places where new life grows."

"At least I know where I'm at, right?" A nervous, yet hopeful voice squeaked out of my throat.

Charm described how plants grow and survive in the desert. "It's hot in the desert," she explained. "It's dry too. But succulent plants such as cacti, aloes, and agaves beat the dry heat by storing plenty of water in their roots, stems, or leaves. God's inviting you into this desert place so you can drink more deeply of the water with which he baptized you and with which he continues to nourish you through the Holy Spirit. Your well's run dry. It's time to let God fill it."

She then told me about the Scripture story of the woman at the well and how Jesus knew her—knew what she needed and desired. The woman came to the well to get a jug of water. After encountering Jesus, she received much more. She experienced the eternal living water of grace.

"That's what I want, Charm. I want more living water and grace. I want to be like those succulent plants in the desert and drink deeply of God's love and wisdom."

"That's why you're here. And like the woman at the well, the Spirit has drawn you here. Your heart is leading you and your feet are catching up."

Charm helped me understand how I'd misread what I experienced at the retreat. I was looking for a quick fix out of my too-full, middle-aged life. God had used my stumbling feet to nudge me into spiritual direction. It's how God often works in our lives—he takes our rough edges and sharpens them into diamonds to help us grow. He leads our feet into green pastures, beside still waters, and restores our souls.

"Our stories are sacred," Charm said, gazing at me with grandmother eyes. "We bring the stories of our lives into spiritual direction each month to break them open, look back over our shoulders through the lens that God sees—our God-lens—and gain greater clarity as we notice the Divine fingerprints in our lives."

"I definitely could use more clarity," I told Charm. "In just our hour together, I have a better understanding of how God is at work in my life. I'd like to schedule another appointment."

I've continued monthly spiritual direction since that meeting with Charm. While life still has its good and bad days, somehow the Spirit has managed to open my heart. I know I'm safe and guided by the Divine. And I have a place each month to view my life through the God-lens with the help of my director.

Like the woman at the well, I thought I needed a jug of water—a change in careers—to fill my empty cup. But God had a better plan in mind. He knew I needed others along the path to blow the dust from my eyes, to help me see through the God-lens. The Creator helped me find another part of my spiritual tribe.

12

Discover the Flow of Spiritual Friendships

Oh, Magoo, You've Done It Again!

My wife and I returned to our empty house after dropping our youngest son off for his freshman year of college. The walls, which once echoed with the clatter of four children, were now quiet. The familiar smell of my son's sweaty socks and dirty T-shirts—that used to send me into a tirade shouting, "Clean your room!"—no longer lingered in the air.

A barrage of thoughts ricocheted around my mind: How did the eighteen years of his life unfold so fast? How do I let him go? What do I do with this hole in my heart? Is this all there is? You raise your kids, give them your heart and soul, and then they do what they're supposed to do—they leave and create a life of their own. I should be proud, and I am. But already I miss punching him in the arm, messing up his hair before he goes on a date, and telling him I love and respect him.

I picked up my son's baseball cap from his bedroom floor and positioned it back onto his bedpost, mumbling, "Suck it up, buttercup. It's time to get on with your life."

Over the next several months, sitting alone in the backyard underneath our willow tree and staring at the harvest moon with a cold beer offered me a place of solace—somewhere to mope and mourn. I recalled: They'd become my best friends. We talked about life, and love, even God, sometimes. They were my running partners, fishing and hunting buds, and dad-let's-go-for-ice-cream delights.

I marveled at my wife, whose tight group of girlfriends had been together since high school. After seeing the *Divine Secrets of the Ya-Ya Sisterhood* movie, they created special hats for each other and proclaimed themselves the Ya-Yas. They shared a unique bond through the many stages of life: birthing children, aging parents, launching kids off to college. I teased my wife that she had more photographs of her and the Ya-Yas around the house than she did of me.

Back then, I had no close friends. Sure, I had gym buddies, guys I'd slam a few beers down with after work, but there was nobody I could talk to about the deeper stuff. Stuff like: How do you deal with fear? Do you ever doubt God exists? How do you know if you're doing it right?

Then I stumbled across a book that changed my empty-nested life.

Spiritual Friendships to the Rescue

I'm not sure how I bumped into it. Somebody might have given it as a gift. I could have found it searching aimlessly online during one of those "where are you God? I'm stuck in a rut" moments.

It was a book by Saint Aelred of Rievaulx, *Spiritual Friendship*,[1] that found its way into my lap one day. In it, Aelred explains that God gifts men and women with one or two special friends whose hearts knit together like Jonathon and

David and Naomi and Ruth. Those friendships form a spiritual bond as God becomes the third person in the relationship.

The words in Aelred's book soothed the loneliness festering inside me. They became an ointment that helped me name the deep yearning I hadn't been able to put into words.

After reading the book, I decided to dive deeper into the topic and make it the focus of my research project for the master's degree in pastoral counseling I was pursuing.

What's a Spiritual Friendship?

Aelred coined the term *spiritual friendships* in the twelfth century. He was the abbot of a monastery and deeply drawn to two other monks in his cloistered community. He confided in them, shared his heart with them. He experienced emotional freedom as they talked about God and laughed and learned together. They became the deepest of friends.

Aelred discerned the friendships were gifts from God and wrote a treatise about them. He looked to the ancient Greeks, Jesus, and the saints to formulate what he called the "doctrine of spiritual friendship."

Philia

According to Aelred, the ancient Greeks counted friendship as a form of love. This virtue, called *philia*, was so esteemed that finding true friendship was the noblest of goals.

Greek philosopher Cicero taught the development of friendship is a natural and necessary part of being human. A type of "second self" develops out of one's friendships, which contributes to the well-being of not only the individual but also society.

For Cicero, true friendship is the second-most important human quality, second only to developing virtue in one's life.

Beloved Friends

From a Christian perspective, Aelred looked to the special bond between Jesus and John as an example of spiritual friendships. Jesus called John the "Beloved." John leaned against Jesus's chest at the end of the Last Supper, exchanging emotional solidarity and strength as they prepared for what lay ahead.

John was the only disciple present at the foot of the cross and to whom Jesus entrusted his mother. John and Jesus were true spiritual friends.

The Friendship Trinity

Aelred defined spiritual friendships as "those relationships which lead [friends] further on the path toward God." This friendship "begins in Christ, is preserved according to the Spirit of Christ...and its end and fruition are Christ."[2]

According to Aelred, like the Holy Trinity, spiritual friends remain distinct individuals formed by and become one in God. God is the third person in the friendship who unites the friends' hearts as they move deeper inward on their spiritual paths.

The essence of spiritual friendships, he says, are two friends with God as their bond.[3]

How Do I Know?

In determining if God has gifted one with a spiritual friend, Aelred points to these four characteristics:

- **Loyalty**. A loyal friend sees nothing but a friend's heart.
- **Right Intention**. The friendship points to and draws both friends to a closer relationship with God.

84

- **Discretion**. They understand what to do for
  each other, what to seek from the friendship,
  and will endure suffering for them. They encourage and gently correct each other's faults.
- **Patience**. The friend accepts correction from the
  other, and patiently endures adversity for their
  friend.[4]

A Book Is Born

After finishing my research paper, I published it as a
book titled *Pillars of Steel: How Real Men Draw Strength from
Each Other*.[5] My face beamed as I watched the book roll off the
printing press.

I celebrated the gift Aelred had led me to name and discover. But joy was short lived when I realized I still didn't have
what I was yearning for—a spiritual friend.

Speed Dating for Friends

All my research didn't tell me how to *find* a spiritual
friend. Paul D. O'Callaghan, who wrote *The Feast of Friendship*,
outlined a modern theology of spiritual friendships but, like
Aelred, didn't give "how-to" instructions.

So, I asked God to lead me to a spiritual friend. I then
started what you might call speed-dating for a friend. I looked
around at the guys in my life, friends from the gym, guys at
work, and the men in my church groups, and asked God if
those guys were the ones the Creator had hand-picked for me
as a spiritual friend.

I had coffee and lunch with some of the guys, even went
for a run with a few, but the minute I talked about God or spirituality, the conversation grew awkward. One buddy I worked

out with at the gym told me flat out, "Guys don't talk about God and faith and feelings. Haven't you heard of the man code?"

"What's that?" I asked.

"It's the unwritten rule that the only topics guys can talk about are sports, cars, and their jobs. Everything else is off-limits."

The man code frustrated me. I decided to make a video proclaiming, "It's time to break the man code!" I posted it on my YouTube page,[6] hoping somebody would see the video and decide they wanted to break the man code, too.

But a spiritual friend didn't show up. So I gave up and stopped speed dating for one.

God Surprises

Several years later, I attended a conference in Chicago. One guy at our lunch table, Ralph, had a surfer-dude way of speaking that I later learned came from living in California for years. As he cracked jokes and we talked as a group about what we were learning at the conference, I felt that familiar twang in my gut, the one that pokes me like a God-nudge.

When the conference ended that afternoon, Ralph asked if I wanted to go get a beer. At first, I declined, but then thought, What do I have to lose? and agreed.

We drank a couple of beers as we talked about the Detroit Tigers and the Chicago Cubs. The conversation eventually flowed into our views about faith and our understanding of God.

"You talk a lot about God," Ralph said in his California surfer-dude voice.

"Yeah. Ever since my dad died when I was sixteen, God's been kind of a big deal for me. He's the one I lean into a lot. Do you believe in God?"

"Sure. I was raised Catholic. But I don't go to church

anymore. I'm spiritual but not religious. And I don't like the word *God*. People use that word too often to beat you over the head with, and I'm tired of all that stuff."

"What name do you like instead?"

"Magoo." Ralph laughed and sat back in his chair. "I like to think of God as Mr. Magoo from the old cartoon series. Whenever the steel beams in my life align, when good things happen, I look up at the sky and say, 'Oh, Magoo, you've done it again!'"

We parted after dinner. Over the next several months, we kept in touch by email and texts. When Ralph lost his job and his father died all within six months, he moved from Chicago to Grand Rapids, where I live.

From that time on, we became the best of friends—spiritual friends. Now we work out together at the gym each day. I've encouraged him to pursue his second career as an artist, and he's encouraged me to grab hold of my dream of being a writer. We've also grown tremendously in our relationship with God as we read, study, and share our unfolding experiences of God's presence in our lives.

Looking back, I realize that just when I was about to give up on God and my desire to find a spiritual friend, God made the steel beams align. He surprised me with Ralph. Aelred gave me an understanding of what was missing in my life, and when the timing was right, God put it all together. I couldn't have planned it better if I tried.

Ya-Ya Wisdom

I still wish there were an instruction manual on how to find a spiritual friend. But I've learned it comes down to deciding you need and want one—so you can become fully human—and then asking God to lead you.

Since my wife and her Ya-Yas have a good track record of cultivating strong friendships, I asked them if they had any advice I could give my readers on how to find spiritual friends.

Here's what they came up with:

- Look around to those currently in your life. Who has God put into your life that might become a true friend?
- Be open and accept invitations when someone invites you for lunch, coffee, a beer, a walk, or whatever. Try on the friendship to see if it's a good fit.
- Act on your own warmhearted impulses, your God-nudges.
- Be intentional about cultivating a friendship. If you seek a true friend, eventually one will appear.
- Join a men's or women's group at church or try out other clubs that interest you. Volunteer doing something you like to do. Notice if there's anyone you meet whom you'd like to know better. Then take a risk and invite them to coffee or lunch.
- Be open to surprises. God often puts people in our lives in unexpected ways. View surprises as the fingerprints of God.
- Pray for a spiritual friendship. Ask and you shall receive.
- Be patient. Finding spiritual friends takes time. But when you find them, they'll point you toward God and your true self.

I wonder how my life would have unfolded had God not surprised me with a spiritual friend. Maybe I'd still be sitting under that willow tree in my backyard staring at the moon, moping. Maybe I wouldn't have become a writer or have learned all the stuff I have about God from reading and talking about the Great Spirit with Ralph. I know I'd be fatter without someone waiting for me at the gym at 6:00 every morning. And Ralph might not have come to call God his best friend.

Aelred says we cannot be happy in this world without committed friendships. His identification of spiritual friendship with the perfect love of God allowed Aelred to make the bold statement, "God is friendship."[7] When you have a true friend, he says, it's a sign and symbol of the divine life of the Trinity—something that allows your life to flow with inner peace, balance, and wholeness.

Ask God for a spiritual friend. Become intentional about looking for one, and I bet the Creator will surprise you. Once you find that friend, STOP: look up at the sky, lift your hands with gratitude, and say, "Oh, Magoo, you've done it again!"

13

Take a Hike!
It's Good Medicine for the Soul

Every Sunday after Mass and a hearty breakfast of eggs and toast, my dad pulled on his hiking boots, grabbed his field jacket, and invited me to join him for a hike in the woods near our home.

Fallen twigs scattering the forest floor crunched under the weight of our boots as we trekked the dirt trails. Swarms of grasshoppers chirped. The smell of decaying crimson, brown, and tangerine-orange leaves filled our nostrils with autumn's scent of musky earth.

I felt safe in the woods walking alongside my father—connected to a nameless Something much bigger than myself. It was as if Dad was teaching me that God speaks to us through nature.

I didn't understand it like that back then. I only knew I adored my father and cherished those times with him in the woods. There was something magical. Sacred. It was almost like the wind and the trees were talking to me.

Later in life, I learned they were.

Nature as Spiritual Practice

In my early thirties, I took a class on nature and spirituality. The professor, Steven Chase, often read excerpts to us students from the book he was writing, *Nature as Spiritual Practice*. "Creation speaks, and the language of creation shapes, forms, and transforms relationships....Every leaf and flower bear the marks and give witness to their Creator,"[1] Professor Chase read from his book.

His words drew me back to those woodland walks with my father. Nature *was* speaking to me back then, I realized. I just needed to learn how to listen and understand the language of Creation.

As part of the class, Professor Chase invited us to take thirty-minute walks around the campus and listen for what the birds, trees, and flowers desired to speak to us. We then came back to the classroom to discuss what we'd experienced.

"Listen with the ears of your heart," he told us before we left for our nature walks. "Let some part of Creation—a tree, a leaf, an insect—find you. Then sit quietly and ask it what wisdom it wishes to reveal to you."

Nature Speaks When We Listen

"A squirrel scampering along the dormitory sidewalk touched the spirit of playfulness within me," one student reported after her nature walk. "I need to stop taking life so seriously. Let myself have more fun."

"I felt one with nature," another classmate offered. "As I sat with my back against an oak tree, I felt my body sway with the tree and the wind. It was a moment of unity, simplicity, and wholeness."

Those were just some experiences that opened my eyes with amazement as I learned the wisdom of nature.

Native American Wisdom

Several years later, my buddy Ralph—who was raised Catholic and Russian Orthodox and is one of the most spiritual guys I know—introduced me to the teachings of Jamie Sams, a writer and artist of Cherokee, Seneca, and French descent. Sams is the co-author of *Medicine Cards: The Discovery of Power through the Ways of Animals.*[2]

According to the Native American tradition, every animal exemplifies a unique spirit or virtue. For example, ant's is patience, cockatoo's is forgiveness, hummingbird's is joy, and parakeet's is hospitality.

The Creator has assigned each creature the task of teaching humans how to integrate its virtue into our lives.

Sams writes,

> Our fellow creatures, the animals, exhibit habit patterns that will relay these messages of healing to anyone astute enough to observe their lessons on how to live. The precious gifts of true medicine [i.e., anything that connects us to the Great Mystery and is healing to the body, mind, and spirit, or that brings personal power, strength, and understanding] are free. Each lesson is based on one major idea or concept and, for the sake of simplicity, each animal has been assigned one of these lessons....When you call upon the power of an animal, you are asking to be drawn into complete harmony with the strength of that creature's essence.[3]

According to Sams, when an animal crosses our path, they become our teachers, if we're open to listen and receive the "good medicine" the Creator offers us through them.

Nature as Part of Community

As I looked back on these threads of nature's teachings, I wondered whether Professor Chase, Jamie Sams, and my dad were showing me how God speaks to us through nature. We are part of Creation's community, and they are part of us.

It's not like an ant ever stopped, shook his finger at me, and shouted, "You need to learn patience!" Rather, when I take time to gaze on those tiny creatures hauling morsels of bread, the ants become a symbol of strength and determination. Despite their size, they possess an immense power, reminding me that nothing comes easy in life without patient effort.

Now, when a particular animal crosses my path, I often grab my smartphone and Google the animal asking, "What's its spirit?" or, as Jamie Sams's refers to it, "What's the animal's totem?"

It's become a fun practice—another way to experience the language of God.

Deer Totem

While sitting at my cottage one day during morning quiet time, a deer appeared on the beach in front of me. I sat watching the doe, marveling at her majestic beauty. When she disappeared into the woods, I went to Google and discovered this:

The meanings associated with the deer combine both soft, gentle qualities with strength and determination:

- Gentleness
- Ability to move through life and obstacles with grace

- Being in touch with inner child, innocence
- Being sensitive and intuitive
- Vigilance: ability to change directions quickly
- Magical ability to regenerate, being in touch with life's mysteries[4]

As I pondered the deer's spirit, I heard the invitation from the Creator to slow down, calm down, and return to the gentle innocence within me.

I lifted the experience up to God with gratitude and asked the Spirit to help me become like the deer. My heart softened. My jaw relaxed. I savored morning coffee as a gentle smile sparkled across my face.

Baptized with Water

Another ritual that nourishes my soul is baptizing myself with lake water. When I go to our cottage, I make a beeline for the beach.

Standing on the shores of Lake Michigan, listening as the waves lap back and forth with the tide, the water's energy draws me with a gentle pull. Savoring the lake's beauty, I lift my nose high and inhale the wisp of air and water mixing in the wind.

I bend down in an act of humble gratitude, cup a handful of water, and bless my head, chest, and legs three times. Wonder flows through my heart as the water and I become one with the mystery of Creation. I'm transformed on the inside as I let go of stress, allowing the Spirit to bathe and cleanse my soul.

Nature's Invitation

Nature invites us to climb her mountains, trek her trails, bathe in her beauty, and listen to the insights animals speak to us through their spirits. When we invite Creation to become part of our community, our hearts absorb the wisdom of wilderness. Take a hike! It's good medicine for the soul.

14

Experience God through Your Body
Discover the Mind-Body-Spirit Connection

Standing in front of my bedroom mirror, an innocent smile lit up my face as I gazed at my nine-year-old body staring back at me. A rush of energy jolted up and down my spine as I caressed my chest, arms, and legs. My fingers stroked the patch of stubbled hair emerging on my chin as I wondered if I was growing from a scrawny boy into a brawny man.

My body is a gift, I thought. A miracle. Each muscle, every bone, all the internal organs work together and form me into a living, breathing human.

Naked in front of the mirror, I turned front to back and marveled at what God had created. I was in love with my body—not in a naughty way—but with pure wonder and childlike playfulness.

Then Mother walked in.

"What are you doing!" she shrieked in that tone of voice that meant *you're grounded*.

"I'm just having fun, Mom. I'm pretending I'm Adam in the Garden of Eden. It's kind of cool."

"Get some clothes on, young man. Wait until I tell your father."

So began the trail of shame that told me my body was bad. Naked was naughty. My flesh was at war with my spirit.

I don't blame Mom for the shame she unwittingly jammed down my throat that day. I later learned she'd had her own body issues as a kid. But I spent the next dozen years wondering what was wrong with me. Why did I enjoy looking at my body? Was I weird?

Theology of the Body

Years later, I attended a workshop put on by a bunch of nuns who had cracked open Pope John Paul II's "Theology of the Body."[1] The nuns were amazed by the groundbreaking approach the pope took in his series of 129 talks he gave from September 1979 through November 1984. So, they offered a weekend of teachings based on the pope's wisdom.

Really? A group of celibate nuns want to spend a weekend talking about the meaning of the human body, sexuality, and *erotic desire*? Crazy, maybe, but I figured I had nothing to lose. I parked my shame in the parking lot at the spiritual life center and walked through the classroom doors into a brand-new understanding about the human body.

The nuns based the workshop around John Paul II's talks and the book summarizing the pope's teachings by Christopher West, *Theology of the Body for Beginners: A Basic Introduction to Pope John Paul II's Sexual Revolution*.[2]

"Oh, my." I giggled as I gathered the workshop handouts. "This is going to be an interesting weekend!"

Sister Roberta, a tall, thin nun with a big, black rosary hanging from her belt and who looked like a penguin in her black and white Dominican garb kicked off the workshop by telling us too many Christians believe our spirits are "good" and our bodies are "bad." But, she said, that's not the church's teaching. Pope John Paul II cleared that up by stating the belief that the body is bad is a heresy known as *Manichaeism*.

According to Christopher West,

> Mani (or Manichaeus), after whom this false teaching is named, condemned the body and all things sexual because he saw in the material world the source of evil. As Christians we believe everything God created is "very good" (see Genesis 1:31). John Paul II summarized the essential distinction as follows: If the Manichaean mentality places an "anti-value" on the body and sexuality, Christianity teaches that the body and sexuality "always remain a 'value not sufficiently appreciated'" (*Theology of the Body*, 45:3). In other words, if Manichaeism says, "the body is bad," Christianity says, "the body is so good that you cannot even fathom it."[3]

Goodbye Heretic

Wow! I've been walking around with a heretic in my head. I breathed a sigh of relief, sat back in my chair, and began to let go of the guilt and shame pent up since the day Mom found me buck naked in my bedroom.

As I sat listening, I realized I'd swallowed a bunch of untruths about the body over the years. The pope and Sister Roberta were giving me a chance to undo that false thinking.

Sister Roberta explained that the human body expresses divine love. She quoted the words of Christopher West: "Love is supremely spiritual, but as Christ demonstrates, love is expressed and realized *in the body*. In fact, God inscribed the call to divine love in our bodies—in our sexuality—right from the beginning."[4]

According to the Catholic Catechism, "God himself is an eternal exchange of love, Father, Son, and Holy Spirit, and he has destined us to share in that exchange."[5]

When we embrace the beauty and dignity of our bodies, we live out Christ's invitation to love God, ourselves, and others with divine love. We participate in the community of human and divine relationships uniting us as "one flesh." We become the kingdom of love here on earth as it is in heaven.

I'd never heard the good nuns at my Catholic grade school tell me what I was learning now for the first time at age thirty-five. I don't remember my religion teacher, Sister Margaret James, teaching me how beautiful the human body was when she caught me staring at Susie Riley's curly red hair and frosted lips. I just remember the sting on my knuckles from the *wap!* of Sister's ruler.

Divine Embodiment

But something changed over the years, I guess. Maybe we all got wiser as God revealed the deeper truths to us about the freedom and responsibility we've been given as his word is made flesh through us. "This is my body, which is given for you," Christ said at the Last Supper (Luke 22:19).

God allowed himself to be enfleshed with a mind, a body, and a divine spirit by coming to earth as a human. If that doesn't teach us that our bodies are good and holy, then I guess we've missed the whole point.

I missed the whole point until Sister Roberta and the pope set me free.

The Mind-Body-Spirit Connection

The other thing I learned at the workshop was that the mind, body, and spirit are meant to be integrated. They work together like a team of horses pulling a buggy.

The mind, unfortunately, gets bossy and tries to be in charge. "Get out of my way. I've got this," the mind says to the body and spirit.

But because the mind's not supposed to work without the help of the other God-given horses, our human buggies get stuck in the sand trap of overthinking.

Sister Roberta taught us that the body is the horse that tames our overly active minds. When we want to quiet our minds and connect with our spirits, we can practice what she calls "body prayer."

Body Prayer

Body prayer takes on many forms. Here are a couple of them Sister taught us:

Breath Prayer. We can close our eyes, take several deep cleansing breaths, and focus on the pure beauty of breathing in and breathing out. Since the mind can hold only one thought at a time, when we shift our attention to our breathing, the mind takes a break and says to the body, "Thanks. I appreciate the help."

Finding Our Feet. Another body prayer Sister taught was to place our feet flat on the floor or ground. Sit quietly. Notice the energy flowing from the earth beneath us up into our bodies. It might feel like a gentle tingle or grounding. She said to recall that the soil beneath our feet connects us to all Creation on God's amazing earth. Like a tree's roots that grow deep into the soil for nourishment and stabilization, we are grounded in God, she said.

Heart Prayer. We can also place our hands on our chests above our hearts. Feel the warmth of blood flowing in and through the heart-space. Notice the gentle beating of the heart. Sister said some traditions teach the heart is the location of the soul. There's a small flame that flickers in our hearts and connects us to the Divine Heart. That's why Christians often depict the Sacred Heart of Jesus as an image of Divine Love. That same Sacred Heart rests in each of us, Sister explained. It's the radiant heart of God's unconditional love and acceptance planted within us like our DNA.

Julian's Body Prayer. A final body prayer we learned at the workshop was one from Julian of Norwich. Julian was a fourteenth-century Christian mystic and theologian who wrote, "The fruit and end of our praying, this is none other than we be oned and like to our Lord in all things."[6] After suffering immense pain, Julian got in touch with her physical body as a pathway to connect with God. She created a body prayer as a simple way to pray without words and integrate mind, body, and spirit.

The four postures of Julian's body prayer are: *Await, Allow, Accept,* and *Attend.* Sister had us stand up at the end of the workshop and practice these body movements.[7]

Await—with hands cupped open extended at the waist, we stand waiting for the presence of God.

Allow—reaching up with our hands lifted toward the sky, we seek deeper awareness and wisdom.

Accept—standing with hands pressed gently on the chest above our hearts, we accept ourselves and others unconditionally. In the quiet, we receive any insights God offers.

Attend—with palms open and hands extended toward the world, we move into the day to do the work God has given us to do.

As I practiced what I'd learned at the workshop over the next several months, I noticed a shift in my perspective. The war between my body and spirit entered a ceasefire. I allowed myself to stand once again in front of a mirror without shame or guilt and express gratitude to the Creator for the beauty of the body.

Now when my mind tries to run the show, I know how to let body prayer free my mind, body, and spirit so they can connect as one with God.

John Paul II's Wisdom

In "Theology of the Body," John Paul II says the human person is defined by three experiences in the original state of innocence with which we're created: solitude, unity, and nakedness.

Solitude. In solitude—alone each day with God—we learn who we are. We discover that our body expresses the Creator's divine love.

Unity. Our original unity tells us we are part of what John Paul calls "the communion of persons." We are one with God and united with all others through the gift of life and love.

Nakedness. Finally, John Paul says, like Adam and Eve, we too were born naked and unashamed. God's plan of love was and is inscribed in our naked bodies. We are created with the deep desire to love as God loves in and through our bodies. And there's no fear or shame in love. We are God's Divine Love embodied in our human flesh.[8]

Sister Roberta and Pope John Paul taught me it's okay to fall in love with my body, not as something I abuse or use to control or manipulate others, but rather as a vessel in which God's love becomes flesh in and through me as the Creator pours more love into the universe.

Find your mind-body-spirit connection through the beauty of body prayer.

Part Four

CONTEMPLATIVE ACTION

contemplative
action

May you respond to the call of your gift, and find
the courage to follow its path.

—John O'Donohue

15

Got Serendipity?
Tap into Your Spiritual Gifts

"I don't know what I'm supposed to do with the rest of my life," I told my sister as I started senior year in college.

Part of me felt called to the priesthood. Another part wanted to go to law school so I could become a lawyer and change the world—stomp out injustice. I'd also fallen in love with a great gal. We talked about getting married someday and raising a family.

I'd wake up at night in cold sweats, overwhelmed with anxiety as I struggled to figure out which path to follow. My sister suggested I meet with her friend to talk through my quandary. Desperate for any guidance I could get, I agreed.

"I'll set up a date for you and Bishop Tom to have dinner," she said.

"What the heck? A bishop? That's sounds scary."

"He's a down-to-earth kind of guy, good at helping people discern their spiritual gifts. I think you'll like him."

The next weekend I had dinner with Bishop Tom. He greeted me at the front door of his townhome with a firm and friendly handshake. His salt-and-pepper hair made me guess he was in his mid-sixties. His *c'mon-in* smile put me at ease.

For the next two hours we enjoyed a laid-back steak dinner, a couple glasses of Burgundy, and a good chat. Bishop shared two pieces of wisdom that resonated with me.

The Tapestry of Life

First, he told me to look at the threads of my life like those of a tapestry so I could discover the underlying pattern of how God was leading me.

I'd met a wonderful woman. We shared a common faith and similar dreams. I'd been accepted to law school.

Those threads, he said, were weaving the tapestry of my life. "You might want to follow them," Bishop Tom suggested.

Spiritual Gifts

The second tidbit he offered was about discovering our spiritual gifts.

Scripture says the church's role is to help people find their unique talents and gifts and then use them to make the world a better place. Unfortunately, Bishop Tom admitted, the church hasn't done a great job of teaching about spiritual gifts, much less giving people the practical tools to discover them.

"I attended twelve years of Catholic schools," I told him. "I don't remember learning anything about spiritual gifts. Maybe I just wasn't listening?"

He summarized what spiritual gifts are and how to discover them.

"A spiritual gift is a charism," he said as I leaned forward in my chair. "They're unique abilities God gives people so they can be powerful channels to create more love in the world and make it a better place. Getting in touch with our spiritual gifts allows us to see the needs of the world in a new way and discover how we can make a difference. When you use your spiritual gifts, you experience inner peace and joy. You live with deeper purpose and meaning. You become a co-creator with God."

Spiritual Gifts Inventory

He suggested I take the *Catholic Spiritual Gifts Inventory* offered by the Catherine of Sienna Institute.[1] It contains 120 questions to determine which of twenty-four spiritual gifts are your top five.

A few days later, I took the *Inventory*. My top gifts came out as: learning, teaching, writing, encouragement, and administration.

It was a cool experience, but I didn't know how to apply the results. After days of scratching my head, I called Bishop Tom and asked him for more guidance.

"Add the Inventory results to the threads forming within the tapestry of your life," he told me. "How do they fit together in a pattern?"

"I guess falling in love with my girlfriend and wanting to have children rules out the priesthood," I chuckled. "And I suppose as a lawyer, I'll get to study the law, help clients follow it, and maybe even do workshops to teach people about a bunch of legal topics and options. That'd allow me to use most of my gifts."

"Then trust your heart and follow it," he said. "Trust the faith that comes before doubt."

His words sealed the deal for me. It was time to trust my gut, take a leap of faith into the future, and enter law school. My girlfriend was relieved.

And Then It's Halftime

For the next twenty-five years, I practiced law, counseled and encouraged a host of clients, taught estate planning workshops, and, with my wife, raised our family. I also volunteered at church and spent time writing in my journal each day. It felt like I was using my spiritual gifts to help others. It was rewarding for the first half of life.

But, as our children launched into college, I felt restless again. Empty.

I wondered if there was more to life than going to work and helping clients. Something was poking at me on the inside. Maybe there was another half of life waiting for me—a second career, I thought. I wasn't sure what it was or how it might look. I just knew something kept bugging me.

I tried to swipe my restlessness away like a pesky fly. I scolded myself, "Why can't you just be happy with your life as it is, right now?" But the nudge—which felt more like an elbow jab—wouldn't go away.

During one of my spiritual direction sessions with Don, he told me to listen to the nudge. Don't push it away. The restlessness might be God tapping you, inviting you to move in a new direction. He suggested reading two books: *Halftime* by Bob Buford and *Falling Upward* by Richard Rohr.

I scoured the books, searching for insight. Buford and Rohr explained there are two halves of our lives. The first half is our survival phase. We go to school, get our educations, find a mate, maybe raise a family, and launch a job or career.

Around age forty or fifty, we get restless. We find the life we're living has become dreary, meaningless. Emptiness and discontent haunt us. Some life event may happen like a divorce, an addiction, or an illness. We question ourselves and try to numb the suffering that often accompanies this transition into the second stage of life.

110

Some call it a midlife crisis. But according to Buford and Rohr, it's actually the Holy Spirit inviting us to move into the second half of life. Buford says this halftime is an invitation—a bump—to move from success to significance.

Unaware of the midlife bump and how to cope with it, many people get stuck in the first half of life. They become disillusioned and angry. They try pacifying themselves by buying a sports car, motorcycle, or new wardrobe, or by chasing a lover.

Like a football game, however, halftime is a natural part of life. It's a time to pause, take stock of our lives, and seek God's guidance to move into the second half. In doing so, we discover we can find deeper fulfillment and wholeness as we discern how we'd like to leave our mark on the world.

At Don's suggestion, and after reading Buford's and Rohr's books, I brushed the dust off the Spiritual Gifts Inventory I'd taken years ago. I asked God to show me where I was being invited in the second half of life.

Surprised by Serendipity

The answer didn't appear overnight. I didn't have a spark of revelation. But as I looked over my spiritual gifts and asked myself what I'd like to do with the rest of my life, the answer unfolded. Serendipity surprised me as God placed a handful of people in my life at exactly the right time.

Discovering the Gift of Writing

A friend who was a professional editor read some of my journal writings and a short book I was penning. He told me I was a writer and needed to pursue my gift to inspire others.

As a result of his encouragement, I started a weekly blog and published a couple of books. The words I wrote seemed to write themselves on my heart, often arising from my morning quiet time.

The Gift of Encouragement

A Dominican sister invited me to enroll in the spiritual direction certification program offered at a local ecumenical spiritual life center.

I took the bait, loved the classes, and launched into becoming a spiritual director.

The Gift of Teaching

I also followed my passion for teaching, gulped, pushed past the fear of failure, and took the risk of offering workshops on a variety of spirituality topics. I had fun creating half-day and weekend offerings from what I'd been learning over the years. *Finding Flow, Listening for God Knows What*, and *Breaking the Man Code to Become a Man* were some of the workshops I gave and continue to offer. They're life-giving for me and, I suspect, for the participants.

Taking the Big Leap

Redirecting my spiritual gifts into these new ventures empowered and excited me as I launched into the second half of life. But fear and self-doubt soon crept back into the marrow of my bones big time.

Like those school bells did when I was a little kid, the fear monster raged at me: Who do you think you are writing books on spirituality and mentoring others? If people knew how flawed you are, they'd never listen to what you have to say. *Give it up!*

Tired of the self-defeating noise in my head, I asked my writing coach, Chad, why the fear monster was raising its ugly head again.

"It's normal. You're bumping into your upper limit," Chad said.

"What's the upper limit?" I asked.

Chad explained that, according to Gay Hendricks in his book *The Big Leap*,[2] when we move out of our comfort zone by stretching ourselves doing something we love—but which is brand new for us—we manufacture thoughts that make us feel bad. It's like we have limited tolerance for life going well.

Hendricks calls it the "upper limit problem," and it happens to all of us. When we hit the upper limit, we do something that stops our positive movement forward.

If we can identify it as fear of failure, also known as the fear of being happy, we can take the "big leap" necessary to push through and get to the other side.

I sighed with relief. "I guess the resistance in me tells me I'm on the right track. I just have to put my head down, keep doing what I'm doing, and push through with courage and conviction."

"You're right," Chad said with a wise-owl look in his eyes. "Maybe ask God for the grace to tear down the inner wall of fear and move forward with love."

Doing It!

During the next several days, I asked God to give me the grace to push through my upper limit. When my insides screamed, "Stop!" I looked up at the sky and asked the Creator to show me how to keep moving forward despite my fears.

Eventually, I grasped the inner courage I needed to keep moving forward in using my gifts to serve.

"I'm doing it!" I shouted one morning with joy. "I'm moving into the second half of life with the spiritual gifts the Creator has given me." I'd found a part of myself that was always there—it just needed time, grace, and unearthing.

When we share our gifts with others, we become fully alive. We experience joy. We find purpose. Fulfillment. And the world becomes a better place.

Look at the tapestry of your life. Let the divine flow of serendipity surprise you. Take time to discover your spiritual gifts, and then use them to make the world a better place, because the universe needs you and your unique gifts. And if you're looking for a Spiritual Gifts Inventory to jump-start your life, there's one at the end of this book.

16

Stop "Shoulding" Yourself

Befriend Your Heart's Desires

"I should go into the office and work today. I should cut the grass. Maybe I should take the kids fishing," I mumbled to my wife.

"You've got a lot of 'shoulds' running around your mind," she replied. "It's Saturday. Can you stop with the shoulding and ask yourself what would be life-giving? What do you *want* to do?"

"I want to take the kids fishing."

"Then do it. Follow your heart's desire."

My wife was right. I get overwhelmed by all the things I think I *should* do. I should clean out the garage. I should go through my closet and donate the clothes I haven't worn in a year. I should stop eating ice cream and lose ten pounds. All the shoulds pile up like a sky-high mountain of ought-to-dos, and I get stuck not knowing which one to do first.

Learning to Should

I wonder when all the shoulding took a hold of me. Maybe it was in grade school when Sister Margaret James rapped my knuckles with her ruler and told me I should work harder to get better grades. Maybe it was my track coach, Mr. Gardner, who yelled I should be able to do fifty sit-ups without lifting my feet off the ground.

Perhaps shoulding took hold of me as a litmus test for life when I pulled my bed pillow over my head and told my dad I wanted to sleep in on Saturday morning instead of going to swim practice. He pulled the pillow away and told me to stop being lazy. I got up and dressed, hating what I should do.

As I listened to my wife, I wondered what would happen if I replaced all the shoulds running around my head and instead asked myself the simple question: "What's my heart's deepest desire?"

Befriending Our Desires

According to theologian Philip Sheldrake in his book *Befriending Our Desires*, desires are not a bad thing. He says many of the great spiritual writers and teachers point to desire as an important pathway for spiritual growth and discernment. According to Sheldrake, befriending our desires is a key that opens the door to inner freedom. When we attend to our heart's desires, we're able to encounter our deepest selves. We discover that our dreams and God's dreams are often the same.

Sheldrake writes,

The journey of desire moves us beyond a sense of seeking to conform to an understanding of the "will of God" that is arbitrary and totally detached from our actual experience of living. Rather, we are drawn ever deeper into God's desiring within our lives and personalities. This is not static, predetermined, or extrinsic to the kind of person we are. God's desiring in us is expressed in and through what we come to see as our deepest desires.[1]

There's an intimate connection, Sheldrake explains, between desire and the spiritual journey. Desire shows up as a positive virtue in both Hebrew and Christian Scriptures. Spiritual classics, poetry, and other literature often explore the role of desire in relation to God, prayer, making good choices, and responding to change. God desired to create you and me, and without that holy desire, we wouldn't exist.

Beyond Pleasure into Bliss

Desire is much deeper than pleasure. Pleasure is a response to a short-lived experience that often satisfies our senses. A big bowl of triple peanut-butter-cup ice cream brings my middle-aged belly pleasure. But when I'm done licking the spoon, I'm soon wondering what I should eat next.

Desire is longer lasting than simple pleasure. It goes to the heart. It seeks wisdom. It often feels like bliss: a state of divine happiness or spiritual blessedness.

I desire a loving and lasting relationship with my spouse, my children, and a couple of good friends. And when I experience the gift of those relationships, I feel an inner warmth, a sense of contentment that catapults into gratitude. I experience bliss.

Desire is a good thing—if we learn to focus it. When faced with a choice, asking ourselves the question "What's my heart's deepest desire?" is the inner compass that helps us navigate life.

In a fight with a loved one, rather than responding with anger, what if we paused, and asked ourselves, "What's my deepest desire right now?"

That simple question helps us refocus. By asking it, we stop and create inner space so we can find the wisdom to love and forgive. We're then able to articulate our needs and listen to those of our loved one so we can negotiate a solution that works for both of us—one that's life-giving for all.

A Spirituality of Desire

Sheldrake invites us to embrace a "Spirituality of Desire." He writes,

Our desires imply a condition of incompleteness because they speak to us of what we are not or what we do not have. Desire is also, therefore, a condition of openness to possibility and to the future. Desires may ground us in the present moment, but at the same time they point to the fact that this moment does not contain all the answers. Clearly, such ideas have a great deal to do with our experience of choice and change. Being people of desire implies a process of continually choosing. Here, once again, desire comes into its own as the condition for discerning what our choices are and then choosing from within the self rather than according to extrinsic demands. Discernment may be thought of as a journey through desires—a process whereby we move from a multitude of desires, or from surface desires, to our deepest desire which, as it were, *contains* all that is true and vital about ourselves.[2]

The problem is we're not taught what true desire is, Sheldrake says. We mask it with surface pleasures like chocolate or possessions, none of which are bad in moderation but which fail to identify that what we really want at our core is God—the experience of being loved and guided by the One who knows us better than we know ourselves.

A spirituality of desire is vital to inner growth because by naming and embracing our heart's desires we encounter our deepest self, that is, the image of God within. Desire draws us like an umbilical cord to the heart of God, and from that place we discover who we are and how we can be a source of greater love in the world.

Ever since that conversation with my wife and reading Sheldrake's book, I've made a vow to stop going down the rabbit hole of shoulds that only bury me in the sand of confusion and frustration. Instead, I'm replacing the shoulds with the life-giving question, "What's my heart's deepest desire?"

Will you join me? Let's stop shoulding ourselves and befriend our heart's desires.

Oh, and if you're wondering—I took my kids fishing that Saturday.

17

Take a Heart-Break
Embrace Your Sacred Heart

A painting of Jesus hung on the foyer wall of our house when I was a kid. It spooked the bejesus out of me when I stopped and stared at it.

Long, wavy brown hair cascaded down Jesus's shoulders. His russet eyes glared at me, making me feel like I'd been caught doing something naughty. His ominous blood-red heart bursting from the middle of his chest made my skin shiver. A tangerine-orange flame flickered in his heart like a burning campfire ember. His index finger rested on his stomach pointing to the Sacred Heart of Jesus.

My mom loved that painting. She recited novenas to the Sacred Heart of Jesus with great devotion. The Sacred Heart was her "go-to" when she prayed.

For me, that icon was mysterious. Spooky. There was something about that finger pointing to Jesus's heart that grabbed me. Why was he pointing to his heart? Was there a secret message he was trying to convey? Is my heart sacred too? I wrestled with those questions a lot as a kid.

I didn't find the answers until I became an adult and stumbled upon the research of the HeartMath Institute.[1]

What's a Heartmind?

The scientists at the HeartMath Institute believe the heart—not the brain—is our operating system. It's the hard drive that runs our human body, and it has a mind all its own. They call it our *heartmind*. When we're anxious or afraid, the heartmind signals the brain to quiet us by releasing oxytocin, the calming hormone. When we need an extra boost of energy to face danger, the heart tells the brain to release adrenaline to supercharge our bodies with strength.

The Institute reports that since the Enlightenment, with its "I think, therefore I am" philosophy, we've been led down the wrong path to believe that our minds operate our human systems. Our minds, however, seek direction and guidance from our hearts. The two operate as a team.

The heart is the operating system of our onboard human computer. The mind is the software application.

The Soul Lives in the Heart

Many faith traditions teach that the heart is the location of our souls. There's a gentle flame behind our heart. If we place our hands on our chest near our hearts, we can feel its warmth. When we move our hand a few inches away from the chest, we can notice the heart's continuous flow of energy. Move our hand to the other side of our chest, and the warmth disappears.

In the Christian tradition, we call that life-giving flame the *Holy Spirit*. Native Americans call it the *Great Spirit*. The Jewish tradition calls the heart the *Place of Wisdom*.

121

Regardless of what we call it, there's a universal belief that we receive insight and wisdom from God through our heart-space. It's the umbilical cord that connects our human hearts with the Divine Heart.

The heart has intuitive power. It acquires wisdom and understanding through deep listening, the type that occurs in prayer, meditation, and contemplation. When we become quiet and focus on opening our hearts, we access the heart-mind. We plug into the lifeline that connects us with our Source to receive affirmation and guidance from the Creator.

It's as if the mind says to the heart, "Hey, I could use some help here." And the heart responds, "I thought you'd never ask."

As I pondered this heart–mind connection, I realized maybe that's why Jesus points to his heart in that picture. He's telling us our hearts are sacred just like his. And while it's great to worship the Sacred Heart of Jesus, we need to move beyond the physical icon and understand our sacred hearts connect us to the Creator. They're the link that unites mind, body, and spirit with God.

The Sacred Heart Practice

Paul Smith from the Integral Christian Network teaches that when our minds get overly bossy and try to run the show, we can use a simple practice that connects the mind and heart. Through this practice, our minds sink into our hearts. The two become one as we connect with and rest in our sacred hearts.

Here's what Smith taught me to do:

I find a quiet place to sit and relax. I close my eyes and place my hand on my forehead.

Then I slowly brush my hand downward—across my eyes, nose, mouth, and throat until it rests on my chest near my heart. I feel the warmth. I notice the energy that flows from the heart—the energy of Divine Love.

I draw attention to my heartbeat. I feel the rhythm of blood pumping in, around, and through my body. It calms me. I experience Presence.

Returning to this practice throughout the day allows me to reconnect with my sacred heart. When I do, my mind becomes still like a placid lake. It's as if a thin red string of Divine Love connects my heart and mind. Sometimes in this gentle embrace of peace, God gives me a word, phrase, or an image filled with simple wisdom that becomes a source of guidance or joy. I reunite with the Source of Being as I discover and live from the sacred heart of me.

Spiritual Practices to the Rescue

Aaron Niequist in *The Eternal Current: How a Practice-Based Faith Can Save Us from Drowning*[2] says his faith stopped working for him when he tried to *think* his way into wholeness.

He discovered intellect alone wasn't enough to deepen his relationship with God. He read and memorized Scripture, but it simply became more words rambling around his mind. He couldn't think his way from his rational brain into a relational experience with God. Niequist felt like he was drowning in his faith.

Then Niequist discovered that our relationship with God has two components: intellect and experience. It's good to use our minds to better understand who the Creator is so we can intellectually know *about* God. But we can get stuck in trying to *think our way to God*. When we do, we're using our minds alone to relate to God.

That's where the heart comes into play. The heart opens the doorway to experiencing our relationship with God. Our sacred hearts allow us to feel the emotion of being fully loved by God. Our hearts allow us to experience things our minds can't fully explain because God is bigger than our intellect.

Niequist says we have to move beyond "spiritual observation and information" and jump into divine participation through *doable practices* that let us experience God-in-us. Spiritual practices come to the rescue of our drowning minds.

Just like we exercise to maintain healthy bodies, so too we engage in regular spiritual practices to sustain healthy souls. There are many spiritual practices we can adopt to exercise our souls. Those practices include centering prayer, eucharistic adoration, the rosary, daily meditation, body prayer, imaginative prayer, prayer walking, nature as spiritual practice, and the sacred heart practice mentioned above.

The important point is to find those spiritual practices that are life-giving for us, that draw us closer to God and our authentic self, and let them become a daily habit just like brushing our teeth or eating.

That picture of the Sacred Heart of Jesus taught me that our hearts are sacred too. They're the place where we encounter God's living presence in our souls.

Like Niequist, until I found practical ways to experience God through my heart, I was stuck trying to intellectualize my way to the Creator. Now I know that to experience the other side of me, to deepen my relationship with God, I need to lean into those spiritual practices that draw me into the Divine Presence so my soul doesn't get flabby.

The next time you notice you're stuck in your mind, with rampant thoughts racing around your head like a bunch of blind mice, stop and take a heart-break.

Take a Heart-Break

Place your hand on your chest near your heart. Take a few deep breaths. Notice the warmth. Feel your heartbeat. Imagine an orange flame flickering behind your heart. Listen. Let yourself experience God's Divine Presence right there as you embrace *your* sacred heart.

A Stroke of Luck... This Is How We Do It!

Discover "Order—Disorder—Reorder" as the Wisdom Pattern for Inner Growth

I was at my cottage relaxing around a roaring campfire, enjoying a few beers with my buddies. It was a perfect night. Good friends. Huge fire. Big Dipper glistening across a starlit summer sky.

Suddenly, my speech slurred. Gibberish garbled from my mouth. "Ehhh. Yaaa. Rrrr." I knew what I wanted to say, but my brain wouldn't connect with my tongue.

I snuck into the bedroom and phoned my wife. "Have you been day-drinking?" She chuckled, not realizing the gravity of the situation.

A panicked ambulance ride to the hospital and a bunch of pokes, pricks, and MRI scans later, I discovered I'd suffered a stroke. A clot had formed in my left carotid artery, pinching off blood flow to my brain.

"What? How? Why me?" I shook my head as the nurse pushed an IV needle into my vein.

At age fifty-seven, my life hurled into chaos. I wasn't sure if I'd live or, worse yet, spend the rest of my days strapped in a wheelchair.

Alone in a sterile hospital bed at midnight that night, the Almighty and I had a talk. It was a let's-get-real, show-me-your-poker-hand conversation with the Creator. I shook my fist. Demanded answers.

"Am I going to die or get another chance?"

"What would you like?" God whispered in the dark.

"I'm not sure," I answered. "Life just threw me a sucker punch. It'd be nice to leave it all behind—get a one-way ticket to heaven. Yet, I'd miss my wife, children, and grandchildren. I'm going to need your courage if you want me to get out of this bed and try again."

The next morning when the doctor brought in the MRI results, I learned something had happened that didn't make medical sense.

"I've not seen this before," he said with a puzzled look on his face. "The front left artery in your neck is completely blocked. Usually, that triggers total paralysis or death. In your case, the right artery pumped hard enough to create new blood streams that crossed over your skull into the left side of your brain. The only part that's damaged is the area that controls your speech. Everything else checks out fine. With time and therapy, you should be back up and running. You're a lucky man."

My eyes popped. My jaw dropped. My exhausted brain struggled to understand. I was relieved the damage wasn't worse, yet my mind cowered with fear: What about my job as a lawyer? How can I communicate with my clients if they can't make *sense* of my words?

Scud Missiles Happen

The strange thing about life is you never know what to expect. One minute you're enjoying a roaring campfire with your buddies, or singing *zippity doo da* while savoring peanut-butter-cup ice cream on the front porch with your kids, or marrying your high school sweetheart, or landing the perfect job.

The next minute, the tough stuff hits you like a scud missile. Your boss fires you, the dog rolls in poop, your mother gets dementia. You suffer a stroke. When life takes aim at you, it shakes your security. Your heart quivers. Your mouth mutters what we all know is true: *life is hard.*

I had lots of time to ponder over the several days I spent in the hospital waiting for more test results. The speech therapy was hard. My mind was jumbled. It felt like all the information stored in the filing cabinets of my brain had been tossed down a staircase and scattered into loose scraps of paper. Nothing made sense.

I slipped in and out of a private pity party.

The Wisdom Pattern

On the second day in the hospital, my perspective shifted. That morning the Creator reminded me of the words of Franciscan priest Richard Rohr: "Order–disorder–reorder."

I'd heard those words before at the Rohr Living School I'd attended a year earlier. I sat up in bed and replayed Rohr's video[1] that outlines this threefold pattern of transformation. I realized the disorder I was experiencing was inviting me to a new season of inner growth.

Rohr says most of us are born with a sense of order and security. Our parents love and provide for us. Our basic needs of food and shelter are met.

Then something happens that throws us into disorder. Our parents divorce or one of them dies. We fall into an addiction.

The disorder is often traumatic, but it's actually intended to catapult us into a new stage of inner growth. If we discover how we're being invited to gain deeper wisdom, we move into reorder. We change. Evolve. In his book *The Wisdom Pattern: Order, Disorder, Reorder*[2] Rohr says this universal blueprint repeats itself in nature and in human life as a perpetual cycle. It's the template for human growth—the growing pains of psychological and spiritual development.

A Perfect Model

Jesus modeled this pattern. For thirty-three years, his life was mostly one of order and predictability as he preached and spread God's love through his healing words and actions.

Then came the disorder of his passion and death. He endured the agony in the Garden, the piercing with thorns, the whipping, and finally the crucifixion. The suffering he underwent showed us that pain—as ugly as it might be—is the necessary springboard for growth and resurrection.

Once Christ pushed through Good Friday, past Holy Saturday, and into Easter Sunday, he created reorder by pouring the light of love and wisdom—the Holy Spirit—into our hearts.

Where Are You in the Cycle?

Our lives reflect this wisdom pattern. We go to school or work. We tend to our daily tasks. There's comfort in the ordinariness of our days. Then something happens that disrupts our lives.

It might be something big: a loved one dies, we get injured, or our marriage crumbles. It might be something less traumatic. We're overwhelmed by life's busyness. Our lives lack purpose. A nameless inner yearning haunts us. Regardless of the size of the disorder, its pain sets in like an ominous gray cloud as we experience loss, confusion, or even depression.

Society teaches us to distract ourselves and numb our pain. According to the blur of television and magazine ads, there's always a magic drink, a pill, a new car, a video game, or some glory-halleluiah seminar that will take away our angst.

But just as seeds have to push through crusty soil and reach for the sun to grow, we too must pass through and move beyond the suffering toward the light to experience inner growth. If we resist the disorder of suffering—try to blot it out or numb it—we stay stuck. And if we cling to the old "order" we've outgrown, we wither like a seed that doesn't get enough sunlight to bloom into a glorious flower.

When we gently push against the desolation by seeking deeper wisdom and connection with God and our Inner Selves, we find the transition—while painful—often leads to a life-giving reordering of our lives. We evolve. Change. Transform. The desolation gives birth to consolation.

A Stroke of Luck

Before the stroke, my life was in order. I had a secure job. My children were growing up steady and strong. My wife and I had a ten-year plan leading to retirement. I even knew that in the second half of life I'd write books and offer spiritual seminars and workshops.

The stroke threw those plans into shambles. I was confused and lost. My brain felt like a milky pan of scrambled eggs.

When jumbled words and phrases poured out of my mouth, I got angry. Hope seemed distant.

Once I stopped resisting and accepted the stroke as part of a new—albeit uncertain—season of my life, God shed clarity on it. I began to understand what was unfolding in my life was a stroke of luck.

As I listened to Rohr's video that second morning in the hospital, I felt a nudge to rethink things. Maybe the stroke wasn't a roadblock. It was an invitation. I sat up in bed and shifted my head to listen deeper as a flurry of thoughts unfurled.

What if I turned the law firm management over to the younger partner I'd been grooming for seven years now instead of when I'm sixty-seven? Maybe God's fast-tracking my second career. What if I worked part-time at the law firm for the next ten years? I'd be able to realize my dream of writing and offering workshops sooner than planned.

It'd take courage—the virtue I'd prayed for the first night in the hospital—to follow the path that seemed to be unfolding. Over the next week, I checked all the discernment boxes by running the idea by my wife, law partners, spiritual director, and financial planner. Each key person gave me the green light that glowed: "Go!"

After six months and sixty-five tedious outpatient therapy sessions to unscramble my brain and regain my speech, I took the leap and began the transition into the second half of my life. My heart burst with gratitude to the God who took my disorder and shaped it into reorder.

Courage Doesn't Always Roar

Life gives us bite-sized spiritual theories like order, disorder, and reorder to chew on. Then we're given the opportunity to put them into real-life practice as we maneuver through the challenges we face and learn how to make life-giving choices.

Understanding and following the pattern of order–disorder–reorder has a lot to do with courage: Courage that's done its homework, that acknowledges our mistakes and learns from them, so we can grasp the deeper understanding life teaches. Courage that doesn't run from fear but befriends it. Courage willing to explore the universal truths and daily practices that give us the ability to live balanced, peaceful, whole lives.

Artist and writer Mary Anne Radmacher says, "Courage doesn't always roar. Sometimes courage is the little voice at the end of the day that says I'll try again tomorrow."[3]

When we look at our lives through the lens of the universal wisdom pattern, we lean into God, who's always there for us with the courage and wisdom needed to push through life's roadblocks.

If our lives are in a season of order, the Creator invites us to continue on our path because it's working. When disorder slams us—either emotionally or physically—pushing gently against it with prayer and inner work allows us to discover what's on the other side of the chaos. Eventually, we enter reorder.

This is how we do it. We integrate the recurring pattern of order, disorder, and reorder by asking ourselves where we are in the cycle. And sometimes in disorder we discover that what seems to be a loss is instead a stroke of luck.

19

Are You a Mystic?
Doable Spiritual Practices for Everyday Living

The word *mystic* has gotten a bad rap over the ages. Some people think it means levitating or sitting on a meditation cushion humming, "*Om.*" Others think it's a term reserved for exceptionally holy men and women like Saint John of the Cross (who wrote passionate love poems about God while imprisoned for years) or Saint Theresa of Avila (with visions of walking up the steps of an interior castle with Jesus).

A mystic is a person who experiences God. With that definition in mind, I'd suggest we're all mystics. We all have unique experiences of God, whether we're aware of them or not. But we aren't taught about them, much less given an opportunity to talk about them, due to fear of being locked up in a mental health facility.

The Tale of Two Fish

The tale about two fish swimming in the ocean might be helpful as a metaphor for determining if you're a mystic.

One fish says to the other, "Isn't this ocean water beautiful?" The other fish responds, "What water?"

Both fish are surrounded by water—they're swimming in it. But only one of them notices the water. He feels it streaming in and through his gills. He experiences the ocean and notices its beauty. The other fish isn't awake. He's unaware of the water and its beauty, even though it sustains him.

You and God Are One

Like the fish, we're swimming in the ocean of God's love. We're created by God and are One in the Divine. Jesus said, "On that day you will know that I am in my Father, and you in me, and I in you" (John 14:20).

What Jesus points to is the relationship we have with God. Like the relationship we have with loved ones and friends, we can't intellectualize our way into that relationship. We can't experience Oneness by thinking alone, because God is beyond our mere intellect. Instead, we need to experience our mental, physical, and spiritual connection with God. We need to awaken to the Divine Flow that sustains us.

Let's Get into the Divine Flow

Spiritual practices are the doorway that awaken us to experiencing God's Presence. They help us get into Divine Flow and sustain us there.

I think of a spiritual practice as any action we regularly undertake that provides an entryway into the path of deeper union with our authentic selves and the Divine. They're like spiritual exercises for our souls. They keep us healthy on the inside. They help us create sacred space so we awaken to the daily presence and guidance of God. Like water sustains fish, God's love sustains us.

Establishing life-giving habits of spiritual practices allows us to enter the room of our hearts and enjoy the bliss of a deeper relationship with ourselves and God.

Who Threw Them Out?

Somewhere along the way, many faith traditions abandoned teaching spiritual practices. They shoved us up into our heads, as if the only pathway to God was through our intellect by following the right rules and performing rituals. There's nothing wrong with using our minds to deepen our understanding of God, but like a fish thrashing on the beach, our hearts and bodies got thrown overboard. We've lost the *experience* of God and are left gasping for spiritual air.

Richard Rohr puts it this way in *What the Mystics Know*:

We have tried to solve today's problems with yesterday's software—which often caused the problem in the first place. Through a regular practice of contemplation we can awaken to the profound presence of the unitive Spirit, which then gives us the courage and capacity to face the paradox that everything is—ourselves included. Higher levels of consciousness always allow us to include and understand more. Deeper levels of divine union allow us to forgive and show compassion toward more and more [people], even those we are not naturally attracted to, or even our enemies.[1]

This One's Just Right

My hope is you'll use the spiritual practices offered here like Goldilocks in the house of the three bears. Try them on to discover which ones are "just right" for you. Once you find them—the ones that are life-giving—I hope you'll incorporate them into daily life so you can experience God in flesh and bones: Mind—Body—Spirit.

A Smorgasbord of Doable Spiritual Practices

My friend Ralph asked me a long time ago, "What are twelve spiritual practices that have been transformative for you?" I told him about the practices in this book, which I'll recap below. These practices keep me in the Divine Flow.

1. Establish a Place and Time for Daily Quiet Time

Create a special place in your home to be alone with the Creator each day. Find pictures and symbols or bring in some things from nature that allow you to experience your sacred space with God. If you're just starting a daily quiet-time practice, set your alarm clock a half an hour earlier than usual. Get up, light a candle, and sit with God for twenty minutes. When your mind wanders, ask God for a word, phrase, or image to center you. Let it become an anchor for your thoughts as you create inner space for yourself and the Creator. Breathe in God's love and guidance in whatever shape and form you experience it. If nothing comes, that's fine. You showed up. Rest in the quiet each day.

You can check out my podcast episode "Why Meditate?" (https://www.youtube.com/watch?v=EtvD0SG-9fU&t=8s)[2] on YouTube to learn more about the benefits of daily meditation. You might also enjoy my podcast episode "How to Start a Meditation Practice" (https://www.youtube.com/watch?v=SWgYAYXWZMg&feature=youtu.be).[3]

2. What's Your Name for God? What's the Creator's Name for You?

Occasionally, ask yourself, "Who is God to me?" Let a word, phrase, or image help you describe the Divine to you. Then, ask the God of Love, "What do you call me?" Let God's response draw you deeper into your unique and awesome relationship with the Creator.

3. Schedule a Play-Date with God

Take out your calendar and mark on it a monthly time when you and God will leave the world behind and play together. Go for a walk, take a bike ride, do whatever is fun and life-giving for you each month. Notice how this time of playing with God allows you to shake off the world and its stress and recharge you with divine energy.

4. Make a Timeline of Your God-Nudges

Take out a large sheet of paper and draw a line on it. Divide the line into decades. For each decade, write down the God-nudges you experienced during that time of your life. Notice also how you responded to them. Did you hear them? Did you resist them or go with the flow and let God lead you? What was the outcome for each of those holy pokes?

5. Read for Thirty Minutes Each Day

Turn off the television and social media and carve out thirty minutes daily to read a chapter in a good spiritual book. Let the book speak to and inspire you as you chew on it throughout the day.

6. Find a Spiritual Mentor

Take a risk and schedule an appointment with a trained spiritual mentor to learn more about spiritual direction. Feel free to reach out to me and set up a time for us to have an initial conversation about this ancient practice. You can also find a mentor near you through the Spiritual Directors International website. Give it a chance by meeting with the mentor at least three times to determine if he or she is a good fit for you. Once you find a suitable mentor, meet with them monthly to discern God's movement in your life.

7. Find God in Nature

As part of your God-date, take time to be outdoors in nature. Walk along a beach or river and feel the flow of the water's energy inside of you. Let a tree, an animal, or some other part of nature find you. Then ask it what wisdom it wishes to speak to your heart. Let that wisdom become a gift from the Creator.

8. Experience Body Prayer

Find a body practice that nourishes you. It could be yoga, Julian of Norwich's body prayer (await, allow, accept, and attend), or some other form of experiencing God through your body, such as taking off your shoes and finding your feet rooted to the floor or ground. Let your body give you the wisdom God wishes to speak to you through it. Check out my guided meditations on www.brianplachta.com as a way of connecting mind, body, and spirit (https://www.youtube.com/watch?v=PqqchXaaRDg).[4]

9. Take a Spiritual Gifts Inventory

Take the Spiritual Gifts Inventory in this book or the one online at www.brianplachta.com. Write down your top five spiritual gifts. Ask yourself how you are already using those gifts and how you'd like to use them in the future. Let your gifts become your guide for how you live and make the world a better place.

10. Embrace Your Sacred Heart

Use the sacred heart practice in chapter 17 to connect with your heart. Embrace the Divine Love of God that radiates within your heart and soul. You can also go to my YouTube page to experience several other guided meditations designed to connect you with your heart-space (https://youtu.be/ 1ryKuusnzws?list=UUG2KulCSXRUML4VVbW8-OPw).[5]

11. "Love You" Prayer

Sit in the quiet, place your hands on your chest near your heart, and feel the warmth of God's unconditional love. As you inhale, hear God whisper, "I love you." As you exhale, respond to God, "I love you, too." You can experience a guided meditation by going to the Love You Prayer video on my YouTube page (https://www.youtube.com/watch?v=SPfaYoT9_iY&feature= youtu.be).[6]

12. Walking Meditation

Take a walk in a park or another favorite place. Focus on this three-part movement as you enjoy your walk and connect with your inner self—mind, body, and spirit. Here's how:

Let Go

As you lift your foot and take a step forward, allow yourself to name and let go of anything that might be holding you back from inner growth.

Ground Yourself in God and the Present Moment

As you set your foot back down, ground yourself in the present moment. Feel the strength and stability of being grounded in God.

Step into Your Future

With the next step you take forward, become aware of your steady movement into the future. The link in the following note below is to a guided meditation to jump-start your walking meditation (https://www.youtube.com/watch?v=Zc7b-BL4C6g&feature=youtu.be).[7]

Let's Do It!

I have been sharing with you in this book how you can overcome fear and reclaim inner peace, balance, and wholeness. Not fake-it-until-you-make-it. The real deal. You can live a fully energized, happy life. A life that's intimate with God. A life that awakens to the depths of your being—your Divine Self. A life that experiences the living presence of the Spirit, who's available for friendship and guidance.

But don't just take my word for it. On this journey of what I call "finding flow," I've met hundreds of other people who've done the same, and they all followed the four specific lifestyle practices I discussed and illustrated in this book.

Sure, some found the peace we're looking for intuitively,

and others did it intentionally, but what it takes to succeed in life and reclaim the peace that surpasses understanding is more than dumb luck. It's a lifestyle I've learned through trial and error and from meeting many wise mentors along the way. This is the same framework I've been teaching my spiritual direction clients and workshop participants for over twenty-five years.

Many people who have struggled with fear and anxiety chose, rather than being overcome by it, to use it as a launching pad to find a pattern for successful living. People just like you. People who found inner peace.

Appendix

Spiritual Gifts Inventory

What's a Spiritual Gift?

God has given each person several unique talents called spiritual gifts that allow us to make the world a better place. When we share our gifts with others, we become fully alive. We experience joy. Purpose. Fulfillment. We co-create with God, bringing love and compassion into the universe.

The world needs you and your unique gifts to build up the Body of Christ. When you discover and use your gifts in life-giving ways, you tap into joy.

Finding Your Spiritual Gifts

Like other presents, it is impossible to appreciate and make use of our spiritual gifts until they have been opened. This Spiritual Gifts Inventory is a tool to help you discover and open up your spiritual gifts by guiding you through three activities:

1. **Scripture Review**: Highlighting Scripture references that both support the existence of spiritual

gifts and identify those that are commonly found in service today.

2. **Self-Assessment Inventory**: A list of sixty questions that will help you identify which gifts you have received in greatest measure.

3. **Discerning How to Use Your Gifts**: When you've finished the Inventory, write down your top gifts. Go back to the document and read the description for each. Then ask yourself how you're using your gifts in practical, concrete ways. Also pray about how you'd like to use them more fully or in different ways. Consider meeting with a spiritual mentor or adviser to discern how God is inviting you to use your gifts in this season of your life; then claim your gifts and put them into practice.

Scripture Review

The Apostle Paul addresses spiritual gifts in three main sections of Scripture: Romans 12; 1 Corinthians 12; and Ephesians 4. Peter also verifies their existence in 1 Peter 4:10. Through these sections of Scripture, we learn that all Christians have been given at least one spiritual gift. The purpose of spiritual gifts is twofold: (1) to unify Christians in their faith and (2) to produce growth within the church, both numerical and spiritual. These gifts are to be used out of love for one another and in service to one another.

We do not choose which gifts we will receive. God bestows them on us through the work of the Holy Spirit.

Not all the gifts identified in Scripture are used in this Inventory. The spectacular gifts (speaking in tongues, healing and miracles, prophecy, bold proclamation from God) and some of the non-spectacular gifts (martyrdom, celibacy) have not been included. Although these gifts exist, they rarely are utilized in the mainstream of life. Since the purpose of discovering and implementing our spiritual gifts is to unify and encourage others through acts of service and charity, only the service-related gifts have been included.

Here's a list of the spiritual gifts in this Inventory:

Administration. The gift that enables a person to formulate, direct, and carry out plans necessary to fulfill a purpose (1 Cor 12:28; Acts 14:23).

Artistry. The gift that enables someone to create artistic expressions that produce a spiritual response of strength and inspiration (Exod 31:1–11; Ps 149:3a).

Discernment. The gift that motivates a person to seek God's will and purpose and apply that understanding to individual and congregational situations (John 16:6–15; Rom 9:1; 1 Cor 2:9–16).

Evangelism. The gift that moves a person to reach out to nonbelievers in such a way that they are baptized and become active members of the Christian community (Matt 28:16–20; Eph 4:11–16; Acts 2:36–40).

Exhortation. The gift that moves one to reach out with Christian love and presence to people in personal conflict or facing a spiritual void (John 14:1; 2 Tim 1:16–18; 3 John 5–8).

Faith. The gift that gives a person eyes to see the Spirit at work and the ability to trust the Spirit's leading without knowing where it all might lead (Gen 12:1–4a; Mark 5:25–34; 1 Thess 1:8–10).

Giving. The gift that enables a person to recognize God's blessings and respond to those blessings by generously and sacrificially giving of one's resources (time, talent, and treasure) (2 Cor 9:6–15; Luke 21:1–4).

Hospitality. The gift that causes a person to joyfully welcome and receive guests and those in need of food and lodging (Rom 12:13; 16:23a; Luke 10:38).

Intercession. The gift that enables one to pray with the certainty that prayer is heard and that when requests are made, answers will come (Matt 6:6–15; Luke 11:1–10; Eph 6:18).

Knowledge. The gift that drives a person to learn, analyze, and uncover new insights regarding the Bible, spirituality, and faith (1 Cor 12:8; 14:6; Rom 12:2).

Leadership. The gift that gives one the confidence to step forward, give direction, and provide motivation to fulfill a dream or complete a task (Rom 12:8; John 21:15–17; 2 Tim 4:1–5).

Mercy. The gift that motivates a person to feel deeply for those in physical, spiritual, or emotional need and act to meet that need (Luke 7:12–15; Luke 10:30–37; Matt 25:34–36).

Music–Vocal. The gift that gives one the capability and opportunity to present personal witness and inspiration to others through singing (Pss 96:1–9; 100:1–2; 149:1–2).

Music–Instrumental. The gift that inspires a person to express personal faith and provide inspiration and comfort through the playing of a musical instrument (Pss 33:1–5; 150; 1 Sam 16:14–23).

Pastoring (Shepherding). The gift that gives one the confidence, capability, and compassion to provide spiritual leadership and direction for individuals or groups (1 Tim 3:1–13; 4:12–16; 2 Tim 4:1–2).

Service (Helps). The gift that enables a person to work gladly behind the scenes to fulfill the work of God's hands (Luke 23:50–54; Rom 16:1–16; Phil 2:19–23).

Skilled Craft. The gift that enables one to create, build, maintain, or repair items (Exod 30:1–6; 31:3–5; Ezek 27:4–11)

Teaching. The gift that enables a person to communicate a personal understanding of the Bible, faith, and spirituality in such a way that it becomes clear and understood by others (1 Cor 12:28; Matt 5:1–12; Acts 18:24–48).

Wisdom. The gift that allows a person to sort through opinions, facts, and thoughts to determine what solution would be best for the individual or the community (1 Cor 2:6–13; Jas 3:13–18; 2 Chr 1:7–11).

Writing. The gift that gives one the ability to express spiritual truths in written form to edify, instruct, encourage, and strengthen individuals or the community (1 John 2:1–6, 12–14; 1 Tim 3:14–15; Jude 3).

Self-Assessment Inventory

This Inventory is an adaptation of the one written by and used with permission from Neal Boese and Patricia Haller. It was produced by the Evangelical Lutheran Church in America (ELCA). The online version can be found at https://www.elca .org/Our-Work/Congregations-and-Synods/Faith-Practices/ Spiritual-Renewal/Assessment-Tools. A PDF version can be viewed at https://download.elca.org/ELCA%20Resource%20

FINDING FLOW

Repository/spiritgifts.pdf?_ga=2.169406181.534664662
.1613492260-1831595036.1613492260. You can also download a copy on my website: https://brianplachta.com/spiritual
-gifts-inventory-download/.

Instructions

For each of the sixty questions that follow, circle the number that corresponds with the response that most closely matches how you perceive yourself.

4=consistently true, **3**=frequently true, **2**=occasion-ally true, **1**=infrequently true, **0**=rarely true

You might also ask a person close to you to score the Inventory with and for you. Their perception of your strengths may be useful in identifying the gifts with which you have been blessed. After responding to each question, turn to the scoring grid to analyze your results.

Questions

4=consistently true, **3**=frequently true, **2**=occasionally true, **1**=infrequently true, **0**=rarely true				
1. When presented with a goal, I immediately think of steps that need to be taken to achieve the desired results.	4	3	2	1	0
2. I express myself through artistic means.	4	3	2	1	0
3. My faith requires me to seek God's will and purpose in all circumstances that arise in my life.	4	3	2	1	0
4. I can convey the gospel message to nonbelievers in ways they can easily understand.	4	3	2	1	0

Appendix: Spiritual Gifts Inventory

4=consistently true, **3**=frequently true, **2**=occasionally true, **1**=infrequently true, **0**=rarely true				
5. I am moved by those who through conflict or sorrow are wavering in faith.	4	3	2	1	0
6. I am certain of the Holy Spirit's presence in my life and the lives of others.	4	3	2	1	0
7. I am blessed by God each day and gladly respond to these blessings by giving liberally of my time and money.	4	3	2	1	0
8. I enjoy meeting new people and becoming acquainted with them.	4	3	2	1	0
9. I know that God hears and responds to my daily prayers.	4	3	2	1	0
10. I feel compelled to learn as much as I can about the Bible and faith.	4	3	2	1	0
11. I am a take-charge person. When others follow my direction, the goal or task will be completed.	4	3	2	1	0
12. When I see a person in need, I am moved to assist them.	4	3	2	1	0
13. I love to sing and enjoy inspiring others through song.	4	3	2	1	0
14. I find joy and express myself by playing a musical instrument.	4	3	2	1	0
15. I am motivated to provide spiritual leadership to those who are on a faith journey.	4	3	2	1	0
16. I like working behind the scenes to ensure projects succeed.	4	3	2	1	0
17. I enjoy working with my hands in a trade or skill that requires considerable experience to perfect.	4	3	2	1	0
18. My great joy is to communicate biblical truth in such a way that it becomes real and understood by others.	4	3	2	1	0

FINDING FLOW

4=consistently true, 3=frequently true, 2=occasionally true, 1=infrequently true, 0=rarely true					
19. When a challenge is presented, I can usually identify an appropriate solution.	4	3	2	1	0
20. I can take a thought or idea and put it into a clear and inspiring written form.	4	3	2	1	0
21. I enjoy organizing thoughts, ideas, hopes, and dreams into a specific plan of action.	4	3	2	1	0
22. I can translate into artistic form what I first see in my imagination.	4	3	2	1	0
23. I have assisted others as they sought to discern whether their personal decisions were helpful and in accord with God's will for their lives.	4	3	2	1	0
24. I enjoy being with nonbelievers and like encouraging them to faith and commitment.	4	3	2	1	0
25. When I know someone is facing a crisis, I feel compelled to provide support and care.	4	3	2	1	0
26. My trust in the Holy Spirit's presence during times when I encounter personal crisis is a source of strength for others.	4	3	2	1	0
27. I manage my time and money so I can give much of it to the work of the church or other organizations.	4	3	2	1	0
28. I am often asked to open my home for small group gatherings or social occasions.	4	3	2	1	0
29. I often become so absorbed in my prayer life that the doorbell or phone can ring and I will not hear it.	4	3	2	1	0
30. Not one day would be complete without biblical study and thought.	4	3	2	1	0

Appendix: Spiritual Gifts Inventory

4=consistently true, 3=frequently true, 2=occasionally true, 1=infrequently true, 0=rarely true					
31. When I am in a group, others will often look to me for direction.	4	3	2	1	0
32. I feel an urgency to provide housing for homeless people, food for those facing food insecurity, and comfort for those in distress.	4	3	2	1	0
33. I have sung before groups and felt a real sense of God's presence.	4	3	2	1	0
34. Playing a musical instrument has been inspiring for both myself and others.	4	3	2	1	0
35. I have responsibility for providing spiritual guidance to individuals or groups.	4	3	2	1	0
36. People tell me that without my willingness to do the unnoticed jobs, their work would be more difficult.	4	3	2	1	0
37. I am good at building, repairing, or restoring things and find satisfaction in doing so.	4	3	2	1	0
38. I want to express my faith by assisting others to discover the truths in the Bible.	4	3	2	1	0
39. People come to me for help in applying Christian faith and values to personal situations.	4	3	2	1	0
40. I often feel moved to write about my thoughts and feelings so others may benefit from them.	4	3	2	1	0
41. I have succeeded in organizing, directing, and motivating people to achieve a goal.	4	3	2	1	0
42. My artistic work has given spiritual strength to people.	4	3	2	1	0

FINDING FLOW

4=consistently true, 3=frequently true, 2=occasionally true, 1=infrequently true, 0=rarely true					
43. In the congregation, I am often asked if a direction being discussed is in accord with God's will and purpose.	4	3	2	1	0
44. I do not find it difficult to share what Jesus means to me with nonbelievers.	4	3	2	1	0
45. Those struggling with life questions have come to me for guidance and help.	4	3	2	1	0
46. I can see great things happening in my congregation and am not derailed by the pessimism of others.	4	3	2	1	0
47. When I receive money unexpectedly, one of my first thoughts is to share this gift through the church.	4	3	2	1	0
48. I enjoy welcoming guests and helping them to feel at ease.	4	3	2	1	0
49. People have asked me to pray for healing in their lives and have evidenced God's healing power.	4	3	2	1	0
50. My study of the Bible has proven helpful to others in their faith journey.	4	3	2	1	0
51. People have said they like to work with me because the task will be successfully completed.	4	3	2	1	0
52. People have been surprised by how at ease I am while working with those suffering in mind, body, or spirit.	4	3	2	1	0
53. I am grateful and humbled that my singing has provided inspiration and hope for others on their faith journey.	4	3	2	1	0
54. Others have told me they were moved by my playing a musical instrument.	4	3	2	1	0
55. People have come to me for spiritual help and I've developed a long-term relationship with them.	4	3	2	1	0

4=consistently true, 3=frequently true, 2=occasionally true, 1=infrequently true, 0=rarely true					
56. When I turn out the lights, take tables down, work in the kitchen, or put chairs away, I feel I have served God.	4	3	2	1	0
57. My knowledge of building maintenance or repair has been a special value to the church and others.	4	3	2	1	0
58. Students have told me I can take the most difficult idea or concept and make it understandable.	4	3	2	1	0
59. When direction is needed at work or in the congregation, I am generally asked for my opinion.	4	3	2	1	0
60. My written work has been helpful to others in understanding life's truths.	4	3	2	1	0

Scoring Grid

For each set of three questions, add together your answers to get a total score. The strongest gift(s) will generally have a total score of seven or more.

Gift	Questions	Three Scores	Total Score
Administration	1, 21, 41		
Artistry	2, 22, 42		
Discernment	3, 23, 43		
Evangelism	4, 24, 44		
Exhortation	5, 25, 45		
Faith	6, 26, 46		
Giving	7, 27, 47		
Hospitality	8, 28, 48		
Intercession	9, 29, 49		

Scoring Grid continued

Gift	Questions	Three Scores	Total Score
Knowledge	10, 30, 50		
Leadership	11, 31, 51		
Mercy	12, 32, 52		
Music–vocal	13, 33, 53		
Music–instrumental	14, 34, 54		
Pastoring	15, 35, 55		
Service	16, 36, 56		
Skilled Craft	17, 37, 57		
Teaching	18, 38, 58		
Wisdom	19, 39, 59		
Writing	20, 40, 60		

Spiritual Gift Cluster

This Inventory begins your journey toward spiritual gifts discovery. Remember that it is not a scientific instrument. Your perceptions will be validated by others and confirmed through prayer and by their use over time. Next, identify your spiritual gift cluster(s).

If you have more than one gift with seven or more, these can be called a "gift cluster." Notice how each gift within the cluster has the potential to compliment and support another. The gifts within the cluster will need to be further explored to determine which ones you have been blessed with.

Draw three overlapping circles. In each circle, write one of the spiritual gifts that had a total score of seven or more. Begin with the center circle, identifying the gift that had the highest score.

In the event of a tie, select the gift you feel you have used effectively in the past or the one you think you might be most effective in. Then fill in the other circles with five of the remaining gifts. This group of gifts is your gift cluster.

Discerning How to Use Your Gifts

Now that you've taken the Spiritual Gifts Inventory, list your top five spiritual gifts.

1.
2.
3.
4.
5.

Do you agree that those are your top spiritual gifts?

- Were there any surprises? If so, what?
- In what specific ways are you currently using these spiritual gifts?
- In what specific ways would you like to use your spiritual gifts in the future?
- How do you feel when using your spiritual gifts?

Further Thoughts and Ideas

- You may want to meet with a spiritual mentor or adviser to ponder your Inventory with them.
- Also, seek the Holy Spirit's guidance through prayer and meditation while evaluating your gifts.
- As you use your spiritual gifts, listen for affirmation from others you trust and love. They will recognize and confirm your spiritual gifts through genuine expressions of approval and thankfulness for a job well done.

- Your spiritual gifts do not appear and disappear as you pass through the doors of your church. The special gifts God has given are with you always. They are meant to also be used in your daily life to bring glory to God and serve the needs of others.
- Make a list of how you're currently using your spiritual gifts or how you wish to use your spiritual gifts in the future. As you do, consider their use at home, with your family; at work, with your colleagues; and within your community of faith and more generally.

Notes

Part One

Introduction

1. EMC Corporation, "84% of People Hold onto an Irrational Fear," PR Newswire, June 29, 2018, https://www.prnewswire.com/news-releases/84-of-people-hold-onto-an-irrational-fear-213298101.html.

Chapter 1

1. Robert Thiefels, *Standing in the Midst of Grace: Essays on Living in Christ Consciousness* (Indianapolis: Dog Ear Publishing, 2017).

2. Mother Teresa, *In the Heart of the World: Thoughts, Stories & Prayers*, ed. Becky Benenate (Novato, CA: New World Library, 1997), 19.

3. Frank Van De Ven, "'Getting into the Flow': What Does That Even Mean?," UX Collective Blog, January 9, 2018, https://uxdesign.cc/getting-into-the-flow-what-does-that-even-mean-58b16642ef1d.

4. Richard Rohr, *Breathing under Water: Spirituality and the Twelve Steps* (Cincinnati: St. Anthony Messenger Press, 2011), 54–55.

Chapter 2

1. Cynthia Bourgeault, *The Wisdom Way of Knowing: Reclaiming an Ancient Tradition to Awaken the Heart* (San Francisco: John Wiley & Sons, 2003), 27–40.

Chapter 3

1. Stuart Brown, "Play Is More than Just Fun," TED, May 2008, https://www.ted.com/talks/stuart_brown_play_is_more_than_just _fun/transcript?language=en.

2. Jennifer Wallace, "Why It's Good for Grown-Ups to Go Play," *The Washington Post*, May 20, 2017, https://www.washingtonpost.com/ national/health-science/why-its-good-for-grown-ups-to-go-play/ 2017/05/19/99810292-fd1f-11e6-8ebe-6e0dbe4f2bca_story.html.

3. Cale D. Magnuson and Lynn A. Barnett, "The Playful Advantage: How Playfulness Enhances Coping with Stress," *Leisure Sciences* 35, no. 2 (March 20, 2013):129–44, https://doi.org/10.1080/ 01490400.2013.761905.

Chapter 4

1. Gerald G. May, *The Wisdom of Wilderness: Experiencing the Healing Power of Nature* (New York: HarperOne, 2007).

2. May, *The Wisdom of Wilderness*, xxiv.

3. May, *The Wisdom of Wilderness*, 19.

4. Thomas Keating, "The Re-Emergence of Contemplative Christianity (with Fr. Thomas Keating and Cynthia Bourgeault)," Facebook Watch, Contemplative Monk, February 6, 2018, https://www .facebook.com/ContemplativeMonk/videos/1519984584717452.

Chapter 5

1. Thomas Keating, "Centering Prayer," Contemplative Outreach, June 3, 2020, https://www.contemplativeoutreach.org/center ing-prayer-method/.

Chapter 6

1. Tania Harris, "How to Hear God's Voice," *God Conversations*, accessed November 28, 2020, https://www.godconversations.com/ hear-gods-voice/.

2. Mother Teresa, *In the Heart of the World: Thoughts, Stories & Prayers*, ed. Becky Benenate (Novato, CA: New World Library, 1997), 19.

3. Paul Smith, "Discovering Your Divine Voice," Integral Christian Network, June 16, 2019, https://www.integralchristiannetwork .org/writings/2019/6/16/discovering-your-divine-voice.

4. Paul Smith, "Discovering Your Divine Voice."

Part Two

Chapter 8

1. Reena Mathur, "5 Benefits of Reading Spiritual and Religious Books," Medium, February 8, 2018, https://medium.com/ @mathurreena98/5-benefits-of-reading-spiritual-and-religious -books-57dc3af60b93.

2. Susan M. Erschen, "Getting the Most from Your Spiritual Reading," *Our Sunday Visitor*, March 31, 2019, https://osvnews .com/2019/03/31/getting-the-most-from-your-spiritual-reading/.

3. Henri J. M. Nouwen, *Return of the Prodigal Son: Story of Homecoming* (New York: Doubleday, 1992), 43.

Chapter 9

1. Mark E. Thibodeaux, *God's Voice Within: The Ignatian Way to Discover God's Will* (Chicago: Loyola Press, 2010).

2. Thibodeaux, *God's Voice Within*, 151.

Chapter 10

1. Rose Mary Dougherty, *Group Spiritual Direction: Community for Discernment* (Mahwah, NJ: Paulist Press, 1995), 35.

2. Richard J. Hauser, *Moving in the Spirit: Becoming a Contemplative in Action* (Mahwah, NJ: Paulist Press, 1986).

3. Hauser, *Moving in the Spirit*, 26–29.

4. Hauser, *Moving in the Spirit*, 5.

5. Vocabulary.com, s.v. "Discerning," accessed November 30, 2020, https://www.vocabulary.com/dictionary/discerning.

Part Three

Chapter 11

1. Jane Howard, *Families* (New York: Simon & Schuster, 1978).

2. "Spiritual Direction," Spiritual Life Center, accessed November 28, 2020, https://spiritlifectr.org/spiritual-direction.

3. Russell Shaw, "Why Not Spiritual Direction?," The Catholic Thing, June 24, 2015, https://www.thecatholicthing.org/2015/06/25/why-not-spiritual-direction/.

4. Saint John Paul II, *Christifideles Laici* (December 30, 1988), http://www.vatican.va/content/john-paul-ii/en/apost_exhortations/documents/hf_jp-ii_exh_30121988_christifideles-laici.html.

5. Larissa Marks, "10 Reasons to Get a Spiritual Director," *Huff-Post*, June 10, 2016, https://www.huffpost.com/entry/10-reasons-to-get-a-spiritual-director_b_575883c4e4b0b6c496003803.

Chapter 12

1. Aelred of Rievaulx, *Spiritual Friendship*, trans. Mary Eugenia Laker (Kalamazoo, MI: Cistercian Publications, 1977).

2. Rievaulx, *Spiritual Friendship*, 53.

3. Rievaulx, *Spiritual Friendship*, 51.

4. Rievaulx, *Spiritual Friendship*, 105–32.

5. brian j. plachta, *Pillars of Steel: How Real Men Draw Strength from Each Other* (Wyoming, MI: Principia Media, 2012).

6. brian j. plachta, "The First Conversation: Pillars of Steel—Having the Courage to Break the Man Code," May 12, 2012, https://www.youtube.com/watch?v=BW3dUnEjMP0&t=54s.

7. Rievaulx, *Spiritual Friendship*, 65.

Chapter 13

1. Steven Chase, *Nature as Spiritual Practice* (Grand Rapids, MI: William B. Eerdmans, 2011), xii–xiii.

2. Jamie Sams and David Carson, *Medicine Cards: The Discovery of Power through the Ways of Animals* (New York: St. Martin's Press, 1988).

3. Sams and Carson, *Medicine Cards*, 13.

4. Elena Harris, "Deer Spirit Animal: Deer Totem Meaning," Spirit Animal Info, June 11, 2020, https://www.spiritanimal.info/deer-spirit-animal/.

Chapter 14

1. Saint John Paul II, "The Redemption of the Body and Sacramentality of Marriage (Theology of the Body)," 1984, https://d2y1pz2y630308.cloudfront.net/2232/documents/2016/9/theology_of_the_body.pdf.

2. Christopher West, *Theology of the Body for Beginners: A Basic Introduction to Pope John-Paul II's Sexual Revolution* (West Chester, PA: Ascension Press, 2009).

3. West, *Theology of the Body for Beginners*, 4–5.

4. West, *Theology of the Body for Beginners*, 28.

5. *Catechism of the Catholic Church: With Modifications from the* Editio Typica (New York: Doubleday, 2003), §221.

6. Julian of Norwich, *Revelation of Love*, trans. John Skinner (New York: Doubleday, 1996), 82.

7. "How to Pray the Body Prayer of Julian of Norwich," 2019, https://www.youtube.com/watch?v=_lKdXykzTXk.

8. Saint John Paul II, "Theology of the Body," 15, 21, 69.

Part Four

Chapter 15

1. Sherry A. Weddell, "Bookstore," Catherine of Siena Institute, accessed June 28, 2021, https://siena.org/bookstore.

2. Gay Hendricks, *The Big Leap: Conquer Your Hidden Fear and Take Life to the Next Level* (New York: HarperCollins, 2010).

Chapter 16

1. Philip Sheldrake, *Befriending Our Desires* (Notre Dame, IN: Ave Maria Press, 1994), 101.

2. Sheldrake, *Befriending Our Desires*, 25.

Chapter 17

1. HeartMath Institute, accessed November 28, 2020, https://www.heartmath.org/.

2. Aaron Niequist, *The Eternal Current: How a Practice-Based Faith Can Save Us from Drowning* (Colorado Springs: WaterBrook, 2018).

Chapter 18

1. Erik Wahl and Richard Rohr, "A Conversation on Order, Disorder, to Re-Order," The Wisdom Series, EP 001, July 14, 2017, https://www.youtube.com/watch?v=9Rd5IAzGfj8&feature=youtu.be.

2. Richard Rohr, *The Wisdom Pattern: Order, Disorder, Reorder* (Cincinnati: Franciscan Media, 2020).

3. Mary Anne Radmacher, "Courage Doesn't Always Roar," June 23, 2016, https://www.maryanneradmacher.net/apps/blog/show/44046084-courage-doesn-t-always-roar.

Chapter 19

1. Richard Rohr, *What the Mystics Know: Seven Pathways to Your Deeper Self* (New York: Crossroad, 2019), 11.

2. brian j. plachta, "Why Meditate?," February 17, 2017, https://www.youtube.com/watch?v=EtvD0SG-9fU&t=8s.

3. brian j. plachta, "How to Start a Meditation Practice," February 11, 2017, https://www.youtube.com/watch?v=SWgYAYXWZMg&feature=youtu.be.

4. brian j. plachta, "Mind–Body–Spirit Connection," September 27, 2020, https://www.youtube.com/watch?v=PqqchXaaRDg.

5. brian j. plachta, "Guided Meditations," https://youtu.be/1ryKuusnzws?list=UUG2KulCSXRUML4VVbW8-OPw.

6. brian j. plachta, "The Love You Prayer," August 27, 2017, https://www.youtube.com/watch?v=SPfaYoT9_iY&feature=youtu.be.

7. brian j. plachta, "Walking Meditation," September 29, 2017, https://www.youtube.com/watch?v=Zc7b-BL4C6g&feature=youtu.be.

About the Author

brian j. plachta is a writer, spiritual director, and speaker. A lay ecclesial minister for thirty-five years, plachta holds a master's in pastoral counseling and is a frequent teacher at workshops, retreats, conference centers, and colleges on a broad variety of practical spirituality topics. He is an adjunct faculty member at the Dominican Spiritual Life Center in Michigan and is the founding partner of Plachta, Murphy & Associates, where he practices law.

brian's passion is helping men and women discover their Inner Compass—the divine voice of wisdom in their souls.

His blog, *Simple Wisdom for Everyday Living*, has thousands of subscribers, and he's been sending a new blog post to his subscribers every week since April 2016. He is also the author of two self-published books: *Pillars of Steel: How Real Men Draw Strength from Each Other* and *Life's Toolbox: Blueprints Included.*

A lifelong learner, plachta is also a graduate of the Rohr Institute for Action and Contemplation and has taken theological courses at Western Theological Seminary and Creighton University. plachta has been a spiritual director for twenty-five years and volunteers at Guiding Light Mission, an addiction recovery center.

He and his wife live in Grand Rapids, Michigan, with their dog, Bailey, and cat, Rascal. Having successfully launched their fourth child, the plachtas are empty-nesters who now enjoy an ever-growing brood of grandchildren.

Learn more about brian and download a copy of his Spiritual Gifts Inventory on his website: www.brianplachta.com.